GOODSON MUMBA

Project Management Excellence

Techniques for Optimal Performance

First edition

ISBN: 9798334415263

*This book was professionally typeset on Reedsy.
Find out more at reedsy.com*

Contents

Preface

In an ever-evolving world where complexity and competition are at their peak, the discipline of project management stands as a cornerstone for achieving organizational success. Whether steering a groundbreaking technological initiative, orchestrating a humanitarian project in a remote region, or launching a new product in a competitive market, the principles of effective project management are universally applicable and critically important.

This book, "Project Management Excellence: Techniques for Optimal Performance," is a comprehensive guide designed to equip project managers—both novice and experienced—with the knowledge and tools needed to excel in their roles. It encapsulates the latest methodologies, best practices, and emerging trends in the field of project management, providing readers with a robust framework to tackle the challenges of modern project execution.

Our journey begins with the fundamental concepts of project management, laying a solid foundation for understanding its significance and core principles. As we progress, we delve into the nuances of initiating and planning projects, exploring techniques for effective communication, risk management, and quality control. Special attention is given to the burgeoning field of Agile methodologies and the integration of advanced technologies like AI and machine learning, which are transforming the landscape of project management.

One of the unique features of this book is its real-world case studies and practical examples, including the story of a water project in Zambia. These narratives offer invaluable insights into the application of project management techniques in diverse contexts, highlighting the adaptability and versatility of these practices.

In compiling this book, we have drawn upon the collective wisdom of seasoned project managers, industry experts, and academic researchers. Our aim is not only to impart technical knowledge but also to inspire a mindset of continuous improvement and innovation among project management professionals.

As you embark on this journey through the pages of "Project Management Excellence," we hope you find the content enlightening and empowering. May this book serve as a trusted companion and a valuable resource in your quest for project management excellence, guiding you towards achieving optimal performance in every endeavor you undertake.

Welcome to the future of project management.

Goodson Mumba

Acknowledgement

I would like to eternally and gratefully acknowledge the Almighty God for the infinite intelligence from His universal mind where we draw from all that we come to know and are yet to know. May I also acknowledge and thank everyone that has played a part in my journey of life in terms of spiritual, moral, emotional and material support.

Dedication

I extend my sincerest gratitude to my beloved wife, Edith Mumba, and our children, Angelina, Lubuto, Letticia, Lulumbi, and Butusho, for their unwavering support and understanding throughout the conception, writing, and eventual publication of this book, despite the sacrifices and challenges they endured.

Disclaimer

1

Chapter 1: Introduction to Project Management

Definition and Importance of Project Management

Michael Carter stood at the edge of the bustling village of Musangu, Zambia, watching as the sun dipped below the horizon, casting a warm golden glow over the landscape. It was his first evening in the country, and the reality of the project ahead weighed heavily on his mind. The air was filled with the sounds of children playing and the rhythmic pounding of women grinding Cassava, but underneath the vibrancy lay the stark reality of water scarcity that plagued the village.

As he observed the scene, Michael recalled the pivotal moments in his career that had led him here. With over a decade of experience in project management, he had overseen numerous successful ventures, but this project—bringing clean, sustainable water to remote villages in Zambia—felt like the most meaningful yet.

The next morning, Michael gathered his new team under a large baobab tree at the center of the village. His team was a mix of local workers, international engineers, and NGO staff, all looking to him for direction. Holding a small whiteboard, Michael began his first briefing.

"Good morning, everyone," he said, his voice carrying a mix of confidence and anticipation. "Before we dive into the specifics of our project, I want to talk about what project management really means and why it's so crucial."

He wrote "Project Management" in bold letters on the board and turned to face the group. "At its core, project management is the application of knowledge, skills, tools, and techniques to project activities to meet the project requirements. It's about taking an idea, a goal, or a need and systematically planning, executing, and overseeing the work to achieve that objective."

Michael paused, letting his words sink in. He saw a few nods and intrigued expressions, which encouraged him to continue.

"Now, why is this important?" he asked rhetorically. "Without proper project management, even the best intentions can fail. Imagine trying to build a house without a blueprint, without knowing how many bricks you need, or without scheduling the work properly. The house might get built, but it would likely take longer, cost more, and be of poor quality."

He could see that his analogy was hitting home. The villagers, familiar with the effort of constructing their own homes, nodded in understanding.

"Project management ensures that we use our resources wisely," Michael continued. "In our case, these resources include not just money and materials, but also time, expertise, and, most importantly, the trust and hopes of the people we're here to help."

He pointed to a map of the village and surrounding areas pinned to the board. "Our project is about more than just drilling wells and setting up water purification systems. It's about improving lives, reducing disease, and giving people the opportunity to thrive. But to achieve these outcomes, we need to manage this project effectively from start to finish."

Michael looked around, seeing the impact of his words. The local workers, who had initially seemed skeptical of this outsider coming to lead them, now appeared more engaged and ready to listen.

"Project management is our blueprint," he said, concluding his introduction. "It's our path to turning a vision into reality, ensuring that we deliver on our promises and create lasting change. Together, we're not just building infrastructure; we're building a future for this community."

As the briefing ended, Michael felt a renewed sense of purpose. He knew the road ahead would be challenging, but with a solid foundation in project management principles, he was confident that they could transform Musangufrom a village struggling for basic necessities into a thriving community with access to clean, sustainable water.

The team dispersed with a sense of shared mission, ready to tackle the tasks ahead. For Michael, this was just the beginning, but he knew that by instilling the importance of project management from the outset, they were already on the right path to success.

Key Project Management Principles

After the morning briefing under the baobab tree, Michael Carter decided to dive deeper into the fundamental principles that would guide their project. As the team gathered again, he sensed the importance of this moment. Establishing a common understanding of key project management principles was crucial for the success of their mission.

Michael cleared his throat and began, "Now that we understand what project management is and why it's important, let's talk about the principles that will guide us through this journey. These principles are the backbone of any successful project."

He wrote the first principle on the whiteboard:

1. Clear Objectives.

"In any project, having clear, achievable objectives is paramount," Michael said, turning to the group. "Our primary objective is to provide clean and sustainable water to the village of Musangu and surrounding areas. But we need to break that down into smaller, specific goals—like drilling a certain number of wells, ensuring the water meets health standards, and training local communities to maintain the systems."

Michael could see some of the local team members nodding in agreement. He continued writing on the board.

2. Defined Roles and Responsibilities.

"Everyone on this team needs to know their role and what is expected of them. Clarity in roles prevents confusion and overlap, which can lead to delays and mistakes. For example, Sarah here," he pointed to an engineer, "will oversee the technical aspects of drilling and water purification, while Joseph," he nodded to a local project coordinator, "will handle community relations and ensure we have the support and cooperation of the villagers."

Sarah and Joseph exchanged a glance, already considering their upcoming tasks. Michael moved to the next principle.

3. Effective Communication.

"Communication is the lifeblood of project management. We must ensure that information flows freely and accurately between all members of the team. This includes regular updates, clear instructions, and listening to each other's concerns and suggestions. We'll have daily briefings to discuss progress and any issues that arise."

Michael paused to let the importance of this principle sink in. He knew that effective communication would be particularly challenging in a culturally diverse team, but it was vital.

4. Risk Management.

"No project is without risks," Michael said, his tone serious. "Identifying potential risks early and developing mitigation strategies is crucial. For instance, we might face delays due to unexpected weather conditions or equipment failures. We need to plan for these possibilities and have contingency plans in place."

He saw a few team members jotting down notes, understanding that their preparation would be key to overcoming obstacles.

5. Quality Control.

"Quality must never be compromised," Michael emphasized. "We are here to provide a sustainable solution. That means every well we drill, every pipe we lay, must meet high standards. Regular inspections and adherence to best practices will ensure that the systems we put in place are reliable and safe."

He moved to the final principle for the day.

6. Continuous Improvement.

"A successful project learns and adapts along the way. We need to constantly evaluate our processes and outcomes, learning from our successes and mistakes. This will help us improve not only this project but also any future projects we undertake."

Michael looked around, ensuring he had everyone's attention. "By adhering to these principles, we set ourselves up for success. They provide a framework that guides our actions and decisions, helping us stay focused on our objectives and navigate the challenges that will undoubtedly come our way."

One of the local team members, a young man named David, raised his hand. "Mr. Carter, how do we make sure that everyone, especially those who aren't here for these briefings, understands and follows these principles?"

"That's an excellent question, David," Michael replied. "We'll create a project charter that outlines these principles and distribute it to everyone involved. Additionally, we'll hold regular training sessions and workshops to reinforce these concepts and ensure that every team member is on the same page."

As the session concluded, Michael felt a sense of accomplishment. The team was beginning to understand the foundational principles that would guide their work. He knew that instilling these principles early on was crucial for fostering a disciplined, motivated, and cohesive team capable of overcoming the challenges ahead. With these guidelines in place, they were one step closer to transforming Musangufrom a community struggling with water scarcity to one flourishing with reliable access to clean water.

The Project Life Cycle

With the principles of project management firmly established, Michael Carter moved on to the next critical topic: the project life cycle. He gathered his team once more under the baobab tree, the village's central meeting spot, its broad canopy providing welcome shade from the midday sun.

Michael could see the team was ready for more. Their enthusiasm was palpable, and he knew the time was right to delve deeper into the structure that would guide their work.

"Alright, team," Michael began, flipping a new page on his whiteboard. "Now that we've discussed the principles, let's talk about the project life cycle. Understanding this cycle is key to managing any project effectively, and it will help us navigate each phase of our water project here in Musangu."

He wrote the phases on the board as he spoke: **Initiation,**

Planning, Execution, Monitoring and Controlling, and Closing.

1. Initiation: "Initiation is the first phase," Michael explained. "This is where we define the project at a high level and determine its feasibility. For our project, this phase included identifying the need for clean water in Musangu and securing the funding and support from our sponsors."

He looked at the team, many of whom had been involved in the preliminary surveys and community meetings. "During initiation, we also set our initial goals and objectives. It's about getting the green light to move forward."

2. Planning: "Planning is arguably the most critical phase," Michael continued. "In this phase, we develop a detailed roadmap to achieve our objectives. This includes defining the scope, setting milestones, allocating resources, and creating schedules."

Michael pointed to a large map of Musangu pinned to the whiteboard. "We've already started some of this work. For instance, we've mapped out where the wells will be drilled and identified the key community leaders who will help us."

He saw the team nodding, and some were even starting to see the bigger picture.

3. Execution: "Execution is where the real work happens," Michael said with a smile. "This is when we actually carry out the plan. We'll be drilling wells, installing water purification systems, and training the villagers."

He gestured to the group. "Each of you will have specific tasks and responsibilities during this phase. It's about following the plan and making adjustments as needed to stay on track."

4. Monitoring and Controlling: "This phase runs concurrently with execution," Michael explained. "While we're working, we need to continuously monitor our progress and control any deviations from our plan. This means tracking performance, managing changes, and ensuring we're meeting our objectives."

He emphasized the importance of vigilance. "We'll use key performance indicators to measure our progress. Regular reports and meetings will help us stay aligned and address any issues promptly."

5. Closing: "Finally, we have the closing phase," Michael said, writing the last word on the board. "This is where we formally close the project and hand over the completed work. For us, this means ensuring the water systems are fully operational, the villagers are trained, and all project documentation is completed."

Michael looked around at his team, seeing a mix of determination and readiness in their eyes. "Closing also involves reflecting on what we've accomplished and identifying lessons learned. This will help us improve future projects and ensure sustainability for the systems we've put in place."

He took a step back, allowing the team to absorb the information. "The project life cycle is a framework that guides us through the complexities of project management. By following these phases, we ensure that our work is organized, efficient, and ultimately successful."

One of the engineers, Sarah, raised her hand. "Michael, how do we handle unexpected issues that arise during the execution phase? For example, if we encounter a problem with the drilling equipment?"

"Great question, Sarah," Michael replied. "That's where the monitoring and controlling phase is vital. We need to be proactive in identifying potential risks and have contingency plans in place. If an issue arises, we address it swiftly, adjust our plans, and keep the project moving forward. Flexibility and problem-solving are key."

He glanced at his watch, noting that they had covered a lot of ground already. "Alright, team, let's take a break for lunch. When we return, we'll dive into the specifics of our project plan and assign roles for the upcoming tasks."

As the team dispersed, Michael felt a sense of accomplishment. They were not just a group of individuals; they were becoming a cohesive unit, ready to tackle the challenges ahead. The framework of the project life cycle would guide their efforts, ensuring that each phase was executed with precision and care. The transformation of Musangu was underway, and with each step, they were moving closer to a future where clean, accessible water was a reality for the village.

Roles and Responsibilities of a Project Manager

After the lunch break, Michael Carter gathered his team once more under the sprawling baobab tree. The sun was now lower in the sky, casting long shadows that provided a cooler, more comfortable environment for the afternoon session. Michael knew this next part was crucial. Understanding the roles and responsibilities of a project manager would set the stage for how they would function as a team.

"Alright, everyone, let's dive into the next essential topic," Michael began, his voice steady and authoritative. "Today, we'll talk about the roles and responsibilities of a project manager. This role is vital for the success of any project, and I want to ensure we all understand what it entails."

He looked around at the attentive faces, feeling the weight of their expectations. Picking up a marker, he began to write on the whiteboard.

1. Leadership and Vision: "A project manager needs to lead the team with a clear vision," Michael started. "It's about inspiring and guiding everyone towards our common goal. For our water project here in Musangu, this means ensuring every team member understands the importance of providing clean, accessible water to the community."

Michael made eye contact with David, the local project co-ordinator. "David, you're a key figure in this. Your connection with the community will help us maintain a shared vision and keep everyone motivated."

2. Planning and Scheduling: "Next, a project manager must excel in planning and scheduling," Michael continued. "We need detailed plans outlining every step, from drilling the wells to training the locals. This includes timelines, resource allocation, and task delegation."

He turned to Sarah. "Sarah, your engineering expertise will be critical in this phase. We'll work closely to ensure our technical plans are sound and executable."

3. Communication: "Effective communication is a cornerstone of successful project management," Michael said, emphasizing each word. "This means keeping the team informed, ensuring that information flows seamlessly, and resolving any misunderstandings quickly."

Michael glanced at his assistant, Laura, who had been helping coordinate the logistics. "Laura, your role in maintaining our communication channels, both within the team and with external stakeholders, is crucial."

4. Risk Management: "A project manager must anticipate

risks and develop mitigation strategies," Michael explained. "This involves identifying potential problems early and having contingency plans ready. For instance, if our drilling equipment fails, we need a backup plan to avoid significant delays."

He saw Sarah nodding, her mind already working through possible technical contingencies.

5. Budget Management: "Managing the budget is another critical responsibility," Michael said, writing the next point. "We need to track expenses, ensure we're staying within our financial limits, and make adjustments as needed. Overspending can jeopardize the entire project."

He nodded to Joseph, the finance officer. "Joseph, your role in monitoring our financial health and providing timely reports will help us stay on track."

6. Problem Solving and Decision Making: "Finally, a project manager must be a strong problem solver and decision maker," Michael concluded. "When issues arise, it's up to us to find solutions quickly and make decisions that keep the project moving forward."

He faced the team, his expression serious but encouraging. "Remember, as project manager, my job is not just to lead but to support each of you. If you face any challenges, come to me. We'll work through them together."

David raised his hand, curiosity in his eyes. "Michael, how do you balance these responsibilities without getting overwhelmed?"

Michael smiled, appreciating the question. "It's about prioritizing and delegating. I trust each of you to handle your respective areas. My job is to ensure everything is coordinated and that we're moving towards our goal. By breaking down tasks and relying on the expertise within our team, we can manage even the most complex projects."

As the session wrapped up, Michael felt a renewed sense of confidence within the group. They now had a clear understanding of what was expected from a project manager and how these responsibilities would shape their work. With this foundation, Michael knew they were ready to tackle the challenges ahead, bringing them one step closer to providing the vital resource of clean water to the people of Musangu.

Common Challenges in Project Management

The late afternoon sun filtered through the baobab leaves, casting dappled light on the gathered team. Michael Carter sensed a growing bond among them. They had learned about the project life cycle and the roles of a project manager, and now it was time to discuss the hurdles they might face.

"Alright, team," Michael said, drawing their attention once more. "Let's talk about the common challenges in project management. Every project, no matter how well-planned, will encounter obstacles. Being aware of these challenges helps us prepare and respond effectively."

He wrote "Common Challenges" on the whiteboard and began with the first point.

1. Scope Creep: "One major challenge is scope creep," Michael began. "This happens when the project's scope expands beyond its original objectives, often without corresponding increases in resources or time."

He noticed Sarah's furrowed brow and clarified, "For instance, if halfway through our project, we decide to add more wells without additional funding or manpower, that's scope creep. It can derail timelines and budgets. We need to stay focused on our initial goals and manage any changes carefully."

2. Resource Constraints: "Resource constraints are another common issue," Michael continued. "This can include a shortage of manpower, equipment, or materials."

He turned to David. "David, remember when we struggled to find enough local volunteers for the initial surveys? That's a perfect example. We need to plan resource allocation meticulously and be prepared for shortages."

3. Communication Breakdowns: "Effective communication is crucial, but it can also be a significant challenge," Michael said. "Miscommunications can lead to errors, delays, and frustration."

He looked at Laura. "Laura, your role in ensuring clear and consistent communication cannot be overstated. We need to maintain open lines and regular updates to avoid misunderstandings."

4. Risk Management: "Managing risks is inherently challenging," Michael noted. "We can't foresee every problem, but we must identify potential risks early and develop mitigation strategies."

He pointed to a nearby well, half-dug but halted due to unforeseen rocky terrain. "When we hit that rocky patch, we had to pause and reassess our approach. That's why having contingency plans is essential."

5. Stakeholder Engagement: "Engaging stakeholders can also be difficult," Michael explained. "This includes keeping sponsors, local leaders, and community members informed and involved."

He turned to Joseph. "Joseph, you've been great at liaising with our sponsors. Ensuring they understand our progress and challenges helps maintain their support."

6. Maintaining Motivation: "Finally, maintaining team motivation over the project's duration can be tough," Michael said. "Fatigue, setbacks, and long timelines can affect morale."

He looked at his team, each person vital to the project's success. "That's why recognizing achievements, no matter how small, and supporting each other is crucial. We're in this together."

Sarah raised her hand, a thoughtful expression on her face. "Michael, what do we do when we face multiple challenges simultaneously?"

Michael smiled, appreciating the question. "Great question, Sarah. When multiple issues arise, it's about prioritizing and tackling them systematically. We assess which challenges are the most critical and address them first. Staying calm and focused is key. Remember, we're a team – we support each other."

He saw nods of agreement and determination. "Challenges are inevitable, but they're also opportunities for growth and learning. By anticipating these issues and planning accordingly, we can navigate them successfully."

The discussion continued, with team members sharing their thoughts and experiences. As the sun began to set, Michael felt a sense of accomplishment. They had not only identified potential obstacles but also reinforced their commitment to overcoming them together. The foundation for their project was solid, built on mutual trust and a shared vision. The journey ahead in Musanguwould be demanding, but they were ready, armed with knowledge and a strong team spirit.

Overview of Project Management Methodologies

As the evening drew near, the air cooled, bringing a gentle breeze that rustled the leaves of the baobab tree. Michael Carter knew this was the perfect time to introduce the final, crucial topic for the day: project management methodologies. The team needed to understand the different approaches to effectively tackle their project.

"Alright, team, let's wrap up today's session with an overview of project management methodologies," Michael began. "These methodologies provide frameworks to guide us through our project. Knowing which to use and when is critical for our success."

He drew a large, clear chart on the whiteboard, each section representing a different methodology.

1. Waterfall: "The first methodology is Waterfall," Michael explained. "This is a linear and sequential approach where each phase depends on the deliverables of the previous one."

He sketched a series of cascading steps. "Think of it as a series of steps. We complete one phase before moving on to the next. This is good for projects with well-defined requirements. However, it's less flexible if changes are needed."

Sarah, who had experience with engineering projects, nodded. "It's like building a bridge. Each phase, from design to construction, follows in order."

2. Agile: "Next, we have Agile," Michael continued, drawing a cycle of iterative loops. "Agile is all about flexibility and continuous improvement. It involves working in short, iterative cycles called sprints, with regular feedback and adjustments."

He looked at Laura. "For our project, Agile can help us adapt to on-the-ground realities quickly. If we find a new challenge while drilling, we can adjust our approach without waiting for the entire plan to change."

3. Scrum: "Scrum is a subset of Agile," Michael said, adding a more detailed loop within the Agile cycle. "It focuses on delivering small, incremental changes through sprints. Each sprint has specific goals and ends with a review."

He addressed David. "David, your role in coordinating these reviews and ensuring that feedback is promptly incorporated will be key if we decide to use Scrum."

4. Lean: "Lean methodology focuses on efficiency and eliminating waste," Michael explained, drawing a flowchart with minimized steps. "It aims to deliver value by streamlining processes and cutting out non-essential tasks."

He turned to Joseph. "Joseph, your financial oversight will help us identify and eliminate any unnecessary expenditures, keeping us lean and efficient."

5. Six Sigma: "Six Sigma is all about quality control and reducing defects," Michael continued. "It uses data and statistical analysis to improve processes."

He looked at Sarah again. "Sarah, your engineering precision will be crucial in implementing Six Sigma. Ensuring our drilling and construction processes are flawless will save time and resources."

6. Hybrid: "Finally, there's the Hybrid methodology," Michael concluded. "This combines elements from different methodologies to suit the specific needs of a project. For example, we might use Waterfall for the planning phase and Agile for implementation."

He saw a light of understanding in the team's eyes. "Given the complexity of our project in Musangu, a hybrid approach might be most suitable. We can plan using Waterfall but remain flexible with Agile and Lean principles during execution."

Sarah raised her hand, curiosity evident. "Michael, how do we decide which methodology to use for each phase?"

Michael smiled, appreciating the insightful question. "Great question, Sarah. We'll evaluate each phase's specific needs and constraints. For detailed, structured tasks, Waterfall might be best. For phases requiring adaptability, Agile or Scrum could be more effective. The key is to remain flexible and responsive."

He saw the team's confidence grow as they absorbed the information. "Remember, these methodologies are tools. Our success depends on choosing the right tool for the job and adapting as needed."

As the session ended and the team dispersed, Michael felt a deep sense of satisfaction. They had covered essential ground, setting a strong foundation for the project ahead. With a clear understanding of project management methodologies, they were better equipped to handle the complexities of bringing clean water to the community of Musangu. The journey was just beginning, but with knowledge and determination, they were ready to face whatever challenges lay ahead.

2

Chapter 2: Project Initiation

Identifying Project Objectives and Scope

As the sun rose over the horizon, casting a golden hue across the landscape, the team gathered once more at the project site in Musangu. Michael Carter stood at the forefront, a sense of anticipation palpable in the air. Today marked the beginning of their journey towards bringing clean water to this community, and it all started with defining the project's objectives and scope.

"Good morning, everyone," Michael greeted, his voice carrying with authority and warmth. "Today, we embark on the first step of our journey: identifying the objectives and scope of our project. This lays the foundation for everything that follows."

He gestured towards a large canvas board, where he would outline their goals and boundaries.

1. Defining Project Objectives: "Our first task is to clearly define our project objectives," Michael began. "These are the specific, measurable goals that we aim to achieve through our project. They provide us with a clear direction and purpose."

He wrote 'Project Objectives' at the top of the board, beneath which he listed their primary goals: to drill and establish wells in strategic locations across the community, to install water purification systems, and to provide training on maintenance and hygiene practices.

2. Establishing Project Scope: "Next, we need to establish the scope of our project," Michael continued. "This defines the boundaries of what will be included and excluded from our project. It's essential for managing expectations and avoiding scope creep."

He wrote 'Project Scope' next to the objectives, and beneath it outlined the specific areas they would focus on: drilling and constructing wells, installing purification systems, training community members, and conducting regular maintenance checks for a period of one year.

3. Aligning with Stakeholder Needs: "Our objectives and scope must align with the needs of our stakeholders," Michael emphasized. "This includes the community members, local leaders, sponsors, and regulatory authorities. Their input is invaluable in ensuring our project's success."

He glanced at David, who had been liaising with the community leaders. "David, your insights into the community's needs and priorities will be crucial in refining our objectives and scope."

4. Setting Deliverables and Milestones: "To ensure accountability and progress tracking, we need to define clear deliverables and milestones," Michael explained. "These are specific, measurable outcomes that mark significant points in our project timeline."

He listed the deliverables, such as the number of wells drilled, the installation of purification systems, and the completion of training sessions. Milestones included the completion of drilling operations in each location and the implementation of maintenance schedules.

5. Identifying Constraints and Assumptions: "Lastly, we must identify any constraints and assumptions that may impact our project," Michael said. "Constraints are factors that limit our options, such as budgetary restrictions or time constraints. Assumptions are beliefs or conditions we assume to be true, such as the availability of suitable drilling sites."

He paused, allowing the team to reflect on the potential challenges ahead. "By recognizing these factors upfront, we can better prepare and mitigate risks as we move forward."

As Michael concluded his presentation, a sense of clarity and purpose filled the air. The team understood the importance of clearly defining their objectives and scope, laying the groundwork for a successful project. With each member committed to their roles and responsibilities, they were ready to take the first steps towards transforming the lives of the people of Musanguthrough access to clean, safe water.

Stakeholder Identification and Analysis

Under the shade of a sprawling acacia tree, the team gathered once more, this time to delve into the intricate web of stakeholders that would shape their project in Musangu. Michael Carter stood before them, a map of the community spread out on a nearby table.

"Now, let's turn our attention to stakeholder identification and analysis," Michael began, his voice steady and purposeful.

"Understanding the needs, expectations, and influence of our stakeholders is vital for the success of our project."

He picked up a marker and began to trace the outlines of the village on the map.

1. Identifying Key Stakeholders: "Our first step is to identify the key stakeholders involved in our project," Michael explained. "These are individuals or groups who have a vested interest in the project's outcome or who may be affected by its implementation."

As he spoke, he listed the stakeholders on a nearby whiteboard: the community members, local leaders, government officials, sponsors, NGOs, and regulatory authorities.

2. Assessing Stakeholder Influence and Interest: "Next, we need to assess the influence and interest of each stakeholder," Michael continued. "This will help us prioritize our engagement efforts and tailor our communication strategies accordingly."

He drew a grid on the whiteboard, with one axis representing stakeholder influence and the other representing stakeholder interest. Together with the team, he plotted each stakeholder on the grid, based on their level of influence and interest in the project.

3. Understanding Stakeholder Needs and Expectations: "Now that we've identified our stakeholders, we need to understand their needs and expectations," Michael said. "This requires active engagement and communication to gather insights and build relationships."

He turned to Laura, their community liaison. "Laura, you'll play a crucial role in this process. Your interactions with the community will help us understand their priorities and concerns."

4. Developing Stakeholder Engagement Strategies: "With a clear understanding of our stakeholders, we can now develop tailored engagement strategies," Michael explained. "This involves determining the most effective channels of communication, frequency of updates, and methods of involvement."

He listed various engagement strategies on the whiteboard, including community meetings, newsletters, social media updates, and one-on-one meetings with key stakeholders.

5. Establishing Feedback Mechanisms: "To ensure ongoing dialogue and feedback, we need to establish robust feedback mechanisms," Michael emphasized. "This allows stakeholders to voice their concerns, provide input, and stay informed about project progress."

He outlined the feedback mechanisms they would implement, such as suggestion boxes, community hotlines, and regular feedback sessions.

6. Incorporating Stakeholder Feedback: "Lastly, we must commit to incorporating stakeholder feedback into our decision-making processes," Michael said. "This demonstrates respect for their perspectives and ensures that our project remains responsive to community needs."

He looked around at his team, a sense of determination shining in their eyes. "By actively engaging with our stakeholders and involving them in our project from the outset, we can build trust, foster collaboration, and ultimately achieve greater success."

As the meeting came to a close, the team dispersed to begin their stakeholder engagement efforts, armed with a newfound understanding of the critical role these individuals and groups would play in shaping their project in Musangu .

Developing a Project Charter

As the afternoon sun reached its zenith, casting long shadows across the ground, the team reconvened in their makeshift office tent to tackle the next crucial step in their project journey: the development of a project charter. Michael Carter stood at the head of the table, a stack of papers and a pen in hand, ready to guide his team through the process.

"Now that we've identified our project objectives, scoped our deliverables, and analyzed our stakeholders, it's time to formalize our project's initiation with a project charter," Michael began, his voice carrying the weight of authority and purpose.

1. Defining the Project Scope and Objectives: "Our project charter will serve as the foundation for our entire project," Michael explained. "It will outline the project's purpose, scope, objectives, deliverables, and key milestones."

He began jotting down notes on a blank sheet of paper, summarizing the project's scope and objectives based on their previous discussions.

2. Establishing Project Governance and Leadership: "In addition to outlining the project's scope and objectives, the project charter will also establish project governance and leadership," Michael continued. "This includes defining the roles and responsibilities of key stakeholders, as well as appointing a project manager to lead the team."

He paused, looking around the table at each member of his team. "Based on your expertise and dedication, I'm appointing each of you to specific roles within our project. Together, we will ensure its success."

3. Identifying Assumptions, Risks, and Constraints:

"Another important component of our project charter is the identification of assumptions, risks, and constraints," Michael said. "These are factors that may impact our project's success and must be carefully considered and managed."

He listed potential assumptions, such as the availability of drilling equipment and the cooperation of local authorities, as well as risks and constraints, such as adverse weather conditions and budget limitations.

4. Defining Project Deliverables and Milestones: "Our project charter will also define the project deliverables and key milestones," Michael continued. "These are the tangible outcomes that we aim to achieve throughout the course of our project, as well as the points in time at which we expect to achieve them."

He outlined the project's deliverables, including the drilling and installation of wells, the implementation of water purification systems, and the completion of community training sessions. He also identified key milestones, such as the completion of drilling operations in each location and the commencement of maintenance checks.

5. Obtaining Sign-off and Approval: "Once our project charter is complete, it will require sign-off and approval from key stakeholders," Michael explained. "This ensures that everyone is aligned with the project's objectives, scope, and expectations before we proceed further."

He passed around the draft project charter for each team member to review, making note of any additional input or revisions.

6. Committing to Project Success: "Lastly, our project charter represents our collective commitment to project success," Michael concluded. "It serves as a guiding document that will inform and direct our actions throughout the entire project lifecycle. With dedication, collaboration, and persever-ance, I have no doubt that we will achieve our goals and bring clean, safe water to the community of Musangu."

As the team signed off on the project charter, a sense of purpose and unity filled the air. With their roles and responsibilities defined, their risks and constraints identified, and their objectives and milestones established, they were ready to embark on the next phase of their project journey with clarity, confidence, and determination.

Feasibility Studies and Business Case Development

As the golden rays of the setting sun painted the sky in shades of orange and pink, the team gathered once again in their makeshift office tent, this time to delve into the intricacies of feasibility studies and business case development. Michael Carter stood at the head of the table, a stack of documents and a projector ready to guide his team through this critical phase of their project journey.

"Now that we've outlined our project's scope, objectives, and governance, it's time to assess its feasibility and develop a robust business case," Michael began, his voice projecting a sense of determination and focus.

1. Conducting Feasibility Studies: "Our first task is to conduct comprehensive feasibility studies to assess the viability of our project," Michael explained. "These studies will help us determine whether our project is technically, economically, and environmentally feasible."

He clicked through a series of slides on the projector, outlining the various aspects that their feasibility studies would cover: geological surveys to assess groundwater availability, environmental impact assessments to ensure minimal ecological disruption, and economic analyses to evaluate the project's financial viability.

2. Analyzing Cost-Benefit Ratios: "As part of our feasibility studies, we'll need to analyze cost-benefit ratios to determine the economic viability of our project," Michael continued. "This involves comparing the costs of implementing the project with the expected benefits it will generate."

He projected a spreadsheet onto the screen, filled with rows of numbers representing the project's anticipated costs and benefits. "By carefully weighing these factors, we can ensure that our project delivers maximum value to the community of Musangu."

3. Developing a Business Case: "Once our feasibility studies are complete, we'll use the findings to develop a robust business case for our project," Michael explained. "The business case will outline the rationale for the project, its expected benefits, and its alignment with organizational objectives."

He began sketching out the key components of their business case on a whiteboard: an executive summary, a description of the project, an analysis of the market and competition, a financial analysis, and a risk assessment.

4. Evaluating Alternative Solutions: "As part of our business case development, we'll also need to evaluate alternative solutions to ensure that we're pursuing the most effective approach," Michael said. "This may involve considering different technologies, methodologies, or suppliers."

He encouraged the team to think creatively and critically as they explored alternative solutions, reminding them that innovation often lay at the intersection of necessity and imagination.

5. Securing Funding and Resources: "Finally, our business case will serve as a powerful tool for securing the funding and resources we need to bring our project to fruition," Michael concluded. "By clearly articulating the value proposition and return on investment of our project, we can attract the support and investment of key stakeholders."

He glanced around the table, meeting the eyes of each team member with a look of confidence and determination. "With thorough feasibility studies and a compelling business case, we can demonstrate the viability and value of our project, paving the way for its successful implementation."

As the meeting drew to a close and the team dispersed to begin their feasibility studies and business case development in earnest, a sense of purpose and anticipation filled the air. With each member committed to their roles and responsibilities, they were ready to overcome any challenges and seize every opportunity to bring clean, safe water to the community of Musangu.

Initial Risk Assessment

As dusk settled over the Musangu village, casting long shadows over the rugged terrain, the team gathered once more to confront the challenges that lay ahead. Michael Carter stood at the front of the room, his gaze steady and determined, ready to guide his team through the process of initial risk assessment.

"Now that we've laid the groundwork for our project, it's time to turn our attention to risk assessment," Michael began, his voice cutting through the quiet evening air. "Identifying and mitigating potential risks is crucial to ensuring the success of our project."

1. Identifying Potential Risks: "Our first task is to identify potential risks that could impact our project," Michael explained. "These risks can come in many forms, from technical challenges to environmental factors to unforeseen obstacles in the community."

He passed around a stack of notepads and pens, encouraging each team member to brainstorm potential risks based on their expertise and experience.

2. Categorizing Risks: "Once we've identified potential risks, we need to categorize them based on their likelihood and impact," Michael continued. "This will help us prioritize our risk mitigation efforts and allocate resources effectively."

He drew a grid on a whiteboard, with one axis representing the likelihood of occurrence and the other representing the impact on the project. Together, the team plotted each identified risk on the grid, allowing them to visualize their potential impact on the project's success.

3. Assessing Risk Severity: "With our risks categorized, we can now assess their severity," Michael said. "This involves evaluating the combined effect of a risk's likelihood and impact on the project."

He led the team through a series of exercises to assign severity ratings to each identified risk, allowing them to focus their attention on the most critical threats to project success.

4. Developing Risk Mitigation Strategies: "Having identified and assessed our risks, our next step is to develop mitigation strategies," Michael explained. "These are proactive measures we can take to reduce the likelihood or impact of a risk, or to respond effectively if it occurs."

He facilitated a brainstorming session, encouraging the team to generate ideas for mitigating each identified risk, from implementing contingency plans to diversifying suppliers to enhancing community engagement efforts.

5. Creating a Risk Management Plan: "Finally, we'll compile our risk assessments and mitigation strategies into a comprehensive risk management plan," Michael said. "This document will serve as our roadmap for navigating potential challenges and uncertainties throughout the project lifecycle."

He tasked each team member with contributing to the risk management plan, ensuring that it reflected their collective knowledge and expertise.

6. Embracing a Culture of Risk Awareness: "Ultimately, effective risk management is not just about developing plans and strategies—it's about fostering a culture of risk awareness and resilience," Michael concluded. "By remaining vigilant and adaptable in the face of uncertainty, we can overcome any obstacles that arise and emerge stronger on the other side."

As the team dispersed for the evening, armed with their initial risk assessments and a renewed sense of purpose, the glow of the campfire illuminated their faces with determination. With each member committed to confronting and mitigating potential risks head-on, they were ready to face whatever challenges lay ahead on their journey to bring clean, safe water to the community of Musangu.

Gaining Project Approval and Buy-In

As the evening breeze rustled through the trees, carrying with it the distant sounds of the Musangu village, the team gathered one final time to tackle the critical task of gaining project approval and buy-in. Michael Carter stood at the front of the room, his demeanor confident and determined, ready to guide his team through this pivotal moment in their project journey.

"Now that we've laid the groundwork for our project, it's time to seek the approval and buy-in of key stakeholders," Michael began, his voice carrying a sense of urgency and purpose. "Their support and endorsement are essential to the success of our project."

1. Engaging Stakeholders: "Our first step is to engage with our stakeholders and communicate the purpose and benefits of our project," Michael explained. "This includes community members, local leaders, government officials, sponsors, and other relevant parties."

He outlined a plan for engaging stakeholders through community meetings, presentations, and one-on-one discussions, emphasizing the importance of transparency, empathy, and active listening.

2. Presenting the Project Proposal: "With our stakeholders engaged, we'll need to present our project proposal in a clear, compelling, and persuasive manner," Michael continued. "This will involve articulating the project's objectives, scope, benefits, and alignment with organizational goals."

He shared a draft of their project proposal, highlighting key sections such as the project overview, goals and objectives, methodology, budget, and timeline.

3. Addressing Concerns and Objections: "During the approval process, it's important to address any concerns or objections raised by stakeholders," Michael said. "This requires active listening, empathy, and a willingness to collaborate on solutions."

He encouraged the team to anticipate potential objections

and prepare thoughtful responses, demonstrating their commitment to addressing stakeholder feedback and ensuring project success.

4. Building Coalitions of Support: "In addition to seeking individual approvals, we'll also need to build coalitions of support among our stakeholders," Michael explained. "This involves identifying influential champions within the community and enlisting their support for our project."

He tasked each team member with identifying potential allies and building relationships based on trust, mutual respect, and shared goals.

5. Negotiating and Compromising: "Negotiation and compromise may be necessary to secure project approval and buy-in," Michael acknowledged. "This requires flexibility, creativity, and a willingness to find common ground with stakeholders."

He coached the team on effective negotiation strategies, such as identifying shared interests, exploring alternative solutions, and maintaining open lines of communication.

6. Celebrating Milestones and Achievements: "Finally, as we gain project approval and buy-in, it's important to celebrate our milestones and achievements along the way," Michael concluded. "This not only recognizes the hard work and dedication of our team but also reinforces our commitment to success."

He proposed a toast to their collective efforts and shared a moment of camaraderie and solidarity with his team, knowing that together, they could overcome any challenges and achieve their shared vision of bringing clean, safe water to the community of Musangu.

As the team dispersed for the evening, their spirits buoyed

by the prospect of gaining project approval and buy-in, they carried with them a renewed sense of purpose and determination. With each member committed to engaging stakeholders, presenting their project proposal, and building coalitions of support, they were ready to navigate the complexities of project approval with confidence and resilience.

Chapter 3: Project Planning

Creating a Project Plan

As the first light of dawn pierced the horizon, illuminating the Musangu Village with a soft golden glow, the team assembled once more, their minds focused on the task ahead: creating a comprehensive project plan. Michael Carter stood at the front of the room, a whiteboard marker in hand, ready to lead his team through the intricate process of project planning.

"Now that we've gained project approval and buy-in, it's time to turn our attention to the next phase of our journey: project planning," Michael began, his voice resonating with confidence and purpose. "A well-crafted project plan will serve as our roadmap for success, guiding our actions and decisions throughout the project lifecycle."

1. Defining Project Objectives and Deliverables: "Our first step in creating our project plan is to define our objectives and deliverables with utmost clarity," Michael explained.

"These will serve as our guiding stars, ensuring that every action we take contributes directly to the achievement of our goals."

He drew a series of interconnected circles on the whiteboard, labeling each one with a specific project objective or deliverable, from drilling and installing wells to conducting community training sessions on water sanitation and hygiene.

2. Establishing Project Scope and Boundaries: "With our objectives and deliverables defined, we must establish clear boundaries for our project scope," Michael continued. "This involves determining what is included and, equally importantly, what is not included in our project."

He emphasized the importance of managing scope creep and maintaining focus on the project's core objectives, cautioning against the temptation to deviate from the agreed-upon scope.

3. Developing Work Breakdown Structure (WBS): "Next, we'll develop a comprehensive Work Breakdown Structure (WBS) to organize and structure our project activities," Michael said. "This will break down our project into smaller, more manageable tasks, making it easier to plan, execute, and monitor."

He led the team through the process of creating a WBS, starting with high-level project phases and gradually decomposing them into smaller, more detailed tasks and subtasks.

4. Estimating Resources and Durations: "Once we have our WBS in place, we'll need to estimate the resources and durations required for each task," Michael explained. "This will help us allocate resources effectively and develop a realistic project schedule."

He distributed spreadsheets and templates for the team to use in estimating labor, materials, equipment, and time required for each task, encouraging them to draw on their expertise and experience to generate accurate estimates.

5. Sequencing and Dependency Mapping: "With resource and duration estimates in hand, we'll then sequence our project tasks and map out dependencies between them," Michael said. "This will ensure that our project flows smoothly from start to finish, with each task building upon the completion of its predecessors."

He facilitated a discussion on task sequencing and dependency mapping, encouraging the team to identify critical paths and potential bottlenecks that could impact project progress.

6. Developing Risk Management Plan: "Lastly, as we finalize our project plan, we'll develop a comprehensive risk management plan to identify, assess, and mitigate potential risks," Michael concluded. "This proactive approach will ensure that we're prepared to address any challenges or uncertainties that arise during project execution."

He urged the team to incorporate risk management into every aspect of their project plan, from resource allocation to scheduling to stakeholder communication.

As the sun rose higher in the sky, casting a warm glow over the Musangu Village, the team set to work with renewed energy and purpose. With each member committed to creating a robust project plan that would guide their actions and decisions throughout the project lifecycle, they were ready to embark on the next phase of their journey with confidence and determination.

Work Breakdown Structure

As the morning sun bathed the Musangu Village in golden light, the team gathered around a large table, their eyes fixed on Michael Carter, who stood at the head of the room, ready to delve into the intricacies of creating a Work Breakdown Structure (WBS).

"Now that we have a clear understanding of our project objectives and scope, it's time to break down our project into smaller, more manageable tasks," Michael began, his voice steady and confident. "This is where the Work Breakdown Structure comes in."

1. Breaking Down the Project: "Our first step in creating the WBS is to break down the project into its component parts," Michael explained. "We need to identify all the tasks and activities required to achieve our project objectives."

He passed out stacks of sticky notes and markers, encouraging each team member to write down a task or activity necessary for the project's completion. With pens scratching against paper and ideas flowing, the table soon filled with colorful notes, each representing a crucial aspect of the project.

2. Organizing Tasks into Hierarchies: "Once we have our list of tasks, we'll organize them into hierarchies based on their relationships and dependencies," Michael continued. "This will give us a clear picture of the project's structure and help us understand how each task contributes to the overall project."

He began rearranging the sticky notes on a whiteboard, grouping related tasks together and organizing them into logical sequences. As the structure took shape, the team marveled at the clarity and coherence of their project plan.

3. Assigning Codes and Identifiers: "To facilitate communication and tracking, we'll assign codes and identifiers to each task in our WBS," Michael said. "These codes will help us reference and cross-reference tasks throughout the project lifecycle."

He distributed copies of the WBS template, with columns for task names, descriptions, codes, and identifiers, and instructed the team to fill in the details for each task.

4. Reviewing and Refining: "Creating the WBS is an iterative process," Michael reminded the team. "We'll need to review and refine our structure to ensure that it accurately reflects the scope and complexity of our project."

He encouraged everyone to scrutinize the WBS carefully, looking for missing tasks, redundant activities, and unclear dependencies. With each iteration, the WBS grew more refined and comprehensive, capturing the essence of their project with precision and clarity.

5. Validating with Stakeholders: "Finally, before finalizing our WBS, we'll need to validate it with key stakeholders," Michael concluded. "Their input and feedback will ensure that our WBS accurately represents the project's scope and objectives."

He outlined a plan for presenting the WBS to stakeholders, soliciting their feedback, and incorporating any suggested changes or revisions.

As the team wrapped up their WBS session, a sense of accomplishment and clarity filled the room. With their project broken down into manageable tasks and organized into a clear and coherent structure, they were ready to move forward with confidence, knowing that they had laid a solid foundation for success.

Scheduling Techniques (Gantt Charts, PERT, CPM)

As the morning sun filtered through the trees, casting dappled shadows on the ground outside the makeshift meeting room in Musangu Village, Michael Carter gathered the team around a large table, ready to explore the intricacies of project scheduling techniques.

"Now that we have our tasks identified and organized, it's time to develop a detailed project schedule," Michael began, his voice carrying a tone of determination and focus. "This will help us allocate resources, track progress, and ensure timely completion of our project."

1. Introducing Gantt Charts: "Our first scheduling technique is the Gantt chart," Michael explained, drawing a series of horizontal bars on a large whiteboard. "Gantt charts provide a visual representation of project tasks, their durations, and their dependencies."

He demonstrated how to create a Gantt chart, with tasks listed along the vertical axis and a timeline spanning the horizontal axis. As the team watched, he filled in the bars to represent each task's duration, illustrating their sequence and overlap.

2. Exploring PERT Analysis: "Next, we'll explore the Program Evaluation and Review Technique (PERT)," Michael continued, switching gears to a different aspect of scheduling. "PERT helps us estimate the time required to complete each project task, taking into account uncertainties and dependencies."

He outlined the steps of PERT analysis, including identifying critical paths, estimating task durations, and calculating project duration and slack. With each step, he emphasized the importance of considering best-case, worst-case, and most likely scenarios to account for variability in task durations.

3. Understanding Critical Path Method (CPM): "Finally, we'll delve into the Critical Path Method (CPM)," Michael said, transitioning to the third scheduling technique. "CPM helps us identify the critical path through our project, which is the longest sequence of tasks that determines the project's overall duration."

He drew a network diagram on the whiteboard, with arrows representing task dependencies and circles representing project milestones. As he traced the critical path through the diagram, the team followed along, gaining a deeper understanding of how task dependencies impact project scheduling.

4. Integrating Techniques for Comprehensive Scheduling: "Each of these scheduling techniques has its strengths and limitations," Michael explained, stepping back to survey the whiteboard filled with charts and diagrams. "By integrating Gantt charts, PERT analysis, and CPM, we can develop a comprehensive project schedule that accounts for both time and resource constraints."

He encouraged the team to apply their newfound knowledge to create a detailed project schedule, using a combination of techniques to ensure accuracy and reliability.

5. Monitoring and Adjusting the Schedule: "Creating the schedule is just the beginning," Michael reminded the team. "We'll need to continuously monitor and adjust our schedule as the project progresses, identifying potential delays and implementing corrective actions as needed."

He outlined a plan for regular schedule reviews, progress updates, and adjustments based on changing circumstances or unforeseen challenges.

6. Ensuring Team Alignment and Accountability: "Finally, it's essential to ensure that every team member understands their role and responsibilities in adhering to the project schedule," Michael concluded. "By fostering a culture of accountability and alignment, we can increase our chances of success and deliver our project on time and within budget."

With a renewed sense of purpose and understanding, the team set to work, applying their knowledge of scheduling techniques to develop a detailed project schedule. As they filled in timelines, estimated task durations, and identified critical paths, they knew that they were laying the groundwork for a successful project outcome.

Resource Allocation and Management

As the sun climbed higher in the sky, bathing the Musangu Village in a warm glow, Michael Carter gathered the team around a table strewn with papers and charts, ready to tackle the crucial task of resource allocation and management.

"Now that we have our project schedule in place, it's time to ensure we have the necessary resources to execute our tasks effectively," Michael began, his voice carrying a sense of urgency and determination. "Effective resource allocation and management are essential for ensuring project success."

1. Identifying Resource Requirements: "Our first step is to identify the resources required for each task in our project schedule," Michael explained, picking up a copy of the schedule and scanning through the list of tasks. "This includes human resources, materials, equipment, and any other assets needed to complete the work."

He tasked each team member with reviewing their assigned

tasks and identifying the specific resources required to execute them, emphasizing the importance of accuracy and attention to detail.

2. Assessing Resource Availability: "Once we know what resources we need, we must assess their availability," Michael continued, his gaze sweeping across the room. "This involves determining whether we have access to the necessary resources internally or if we need to acquire them externally."

He encouraged the team to reach out to relevant departments, suppliers, and stakeholders to confirm resource availability and explore alternative options if needed.

3. Allocating Resources Effectively: "With resource requirements and availability established, our next step is to allocate resources effectively," Michael said, drawing a grid on a whiteboard to represent resource allocation. "This involves assigning specific resources to each task in our project schedule, taking into account factors such as skill level, availability, and workload."

He led a discussion on the principles of effective resource allocation, highlighting the importance of balancing workload, optimizing resource utilization, and avoiding overallocation or underutilization.

4. Managing Resource Constraints: "Throughout the project, we'll need to manage resource constraints and conflicts as they arise," Michael acknowledged, his brow furrowing with concern. "This may involve renegotiating priorities, reallocating resources, or seeking additional support from stakeholders."

He urged the team to remain flexible and adaptable in their approach to resource management, emphasizing the importance of open communication and collaboration to resolve issues quickly and effectively.

5. Monitoring Resource Utilization: "To ensure we're using our resources efficiently, we must monitor resource utilization throughout the project," Michael continued, his tone firm and resolute. "This involves tracking resource usage against the project schedule, identifying any deviations or inefficiencies, and taking corrective action as needed."

He outlined a plan for regular resource monitoring and reporting, with designated team members responsible for tracking resource usage and flagging any issues or concerns.

6. Optimizing Resource Management Processes: "Finally, we must continuously seek ways to optimize our resource management processes," Michael concluded, his voice ringing with determination. "This includes identifying opportunities for automation, streamlining workflows, and implementing best practices to improve efficiency and effectiveness."

He challenged the team to think creatively and proactively about resource management, empowering them to drive positive change and maximize the impact of their efforts.

As the team dispersed to begin their resource allocation and management tasks, a sense of purpose and determination filled the room. With their collective expertise and commitment to excellence, they were ready to overcome any challenges and ensure the successful execution of their project.

Budgeting and Cost Estimation

As the day progressed and the sun reached its zenith, casting a warm glow over the Musangu Village, Michael Carter gathered the team once more, this time to delve into the critical task of budgeting and cost estimation.

"Now that we have our project schedule and resource allocation plan in place, it's time to turn our attention to the financial aspects of our project," Michael began, his voice infused with a sense of purpose and determination. "Budgeting and cost estimation are essential for ensuring that we can execute our project within the available resources and funding."

1. Understanding Cost Components: "Our first step is to understand the various cost components involved in our project," Michael explained, gesturing to a whiteboard where he had listed items such as labor, materials, equipment, overhead costs, and contingencies. "Each of these elements contributes to the overall project budget, and it's essential to account for them accurately."

He encouraged the team to consider both direct and indirect costs, as well as any unforeseen expenses that might arise during project execution.

2. Estimating Costs for Each Task: "With a clear understanding of our cost components, we can begin estimating costs for each task in our project schedule," Michael continued, picking up a copy of the schedule and scanning through the list of tasks. "This involves breaking down the resources required for each task and calculating the associated costs based on current market rates and historical data."

He tasked the team with estimating costs for their assigned tasks, reminding them to consider factors such as labor rates, material prices, equipment rental fees, and any other relevant expenses.

3. Developing the Project Budget: "Once we have cost estimates for each task, we can aggregate them to develop the project budget," Michael said, drawing a large table on the whiteboard to represent the budget breakdown. "This will provide us with a comprehensive overview of our project's financial requirements, including total costs, funding sources, and budget allocations for each cost category."

He led the team through the process of developing the project budget, allocating funds to various cost categories and ensuring that the budget aligned with the project scope and objectives.

4. Incorporating Contingency Planning: "No project is without its risks and uncertainties, so it's crucial to incorporate contingency planning into our budgeting process," Michael emphasized, his tone serious and focused. "This involves setting aside a portion of the budget to cover unexpected expenses or changes in project scope, ensuring that we have the flexibility to adapt to unforeseen circumstances."

He urged the team to allocate contingency funds prudently, balancing the need for risk mitigation with the imperative of fiscal responsibility.

5. Monitoring and Controlling Costs: "Once the project is underway, we'll need to monitor and control costs closely to ensure that we stay within budget," Michael continued, his gaze sweeping across the room. "This involves tracking actual expenditures against the budget, identifying any deviations or variances, and taking corrective action as needed to keep costs in check."

He outlined a plan for regular budget reviews, expense tracking, and cost analysis, with designated team members responsible for monitoring and controlling costs throughout the project lifecycle.

6. Communicating Budget Status: "Finally, we must ensure transparent communication regarding the project budget status with key stakeholders," Michael concluded, his voice carrying a note of authority and assurance. "This includes providing regular updates on budget performance, highlighting any significant variances or trends, and seeking approval for budget revisions as necessary."

He emphasized the importance of open and honest communication to build trust and accountability among project stakeholders, ensuring alignment and support for budget-related decisions.

As the team absorbed Michael's guidance and prepared to embark on the budgeting and cost estimation process, a sense of clarity and purpose filled the room. With their collective expertise and commitment to financial stewardship, they were ready to navigate the financial complexities of their project with confidence and determination.

Risk Management Planning

As the golden light of the afternoon sun bathed the Musangu Village in warmth, Michael Carter convened the team once again, this time to address the critical task of risk management planning.

"Now that we have our project schedule, resource allocation plan, and budget in place, it's time to turn our attention to identifying and mitigating potential risks," Michael began, his voice resonating with a sense of urgency and purpose. "Risk management planning is essential for anticipating and addressing uncertainties that could impact our project's success."

1. Identifying Project Risks: "Our first step is to identify potential risks that could arise during the course of our project," Michael explained, his eyes scanning the attentive faces of his team members. "This includes both internal and external factors that could affect our project objectives, timelines, or budget."

He encouraged the team to brainstorm potential risks collaboratively, drawing on their collective expertise and experience to identify a comprehensive list of threats and opportunities.

2. Assessing Risk Impact and Probability: "Once we have identified potential risks, we need to assess their impact and probability," Michael continued, his brow furrowing with concentration. "This involves evaluating the potential consequences of each risk and the likelihood of it occurring, using qualitative and quantitative analysis techniques."

He led the team through a risk assessment exercise, prioritizing risks based on their severity and likelihood and highlighting those with the greatest potential impact on the project.

3. Developing Risk Response Strategies: "With our risks identified and assessed, we can develop appropriate response strategies to address them," Michael said, picking up a marker to sketch a risk response matrix on a whiteboard. "This matrix will help us categorize risks based on their likelihood and impact, and determine the most effective response strategy for each."

He encouraged the team to consider a range of response options, including risk avoidance, mitigation, transfer, or acceptance, tailoring their approach to the specific characteristics of each risk.

4. Implementing Risk Mitigation Measures: "Once we have defined our risk response strategies, it's time to implement risk mitigation measures," Michael continued, his voice brimming with determination. "This may involve taking proactive steps to prevent risks from occurring, or developing contingency plans to minimize their impact if they do."

He assigned responsibility for implementing risk mitigation measures to specific team members, ensuring accountability and follow-through.

5. Monitoring and Controlling Risks: "Throughout the project lifecycle, we must continuously monitor and control risks to ensure they are effectively managed," Michael emphasized, his tone serious and focused. "This involves tracking the status of identified risks, assessing their ongoing impact and probability, and adjusting our response strategies as needed."

He outlined a plan for regular risk reviews, risk reporting, and risk reassessment, with designated team members responsible for monitoring and controlling risks throughout the project.

6. Fostering a Culture of Risk Awareness and Management: "Finally, we must foster a culture of risk awareness and management within our team," Michael concluded, his voice carrying a note of conviction. "This means encouraging open communication, sharing lessons learned, and empowering team members to identify and address risks proactively."

He challenged the team to embrace risk management as a fundamental aspect of their project approach, recognizing that by effectively managing risks, they could mitigate potential threats and capitalize on opportunities to enhance project success.

As the team absorbed Michael's guidance and prepared to embark on their risk management planning journey, a sense of resolve and determination filled the room. With their collective expertise and commitment to proactive risk management, they were ready to confront the uncertainties of their project with confidence and resilience.

Chapter 4: Agile Project Management

Principles of Agile Methodologies

As the evening descended upon the bustling city of Lusaka, casting long shadows across the landscape, Michael Carter gathered his team in a cozy conference room to delve into the world of Agile project management.

"Now that we have a solid foundation in traditional project management practices, it's time to explore the principles of Agile methodologies," Michael began, his voice filled with enthusiasm and anticipation. "Agile is a flexible and iterative approach to project management that emphasizes collaboration, adaptability, and delivering value to the customer."

1. Embracing Change: "Our first principle of Agile is embracing change," Michael explained, pacing back and forth in front of a whiteboard adorned with colorful diagrams. "Unlike traditional project management methods that resist change, Agile welcomes it as a natural and inevitable part of the process."

He encouraged the team to adopt a mindset of flexibility and adaptability, empowering them to respond to changing requirements and priorities in a proactive and constructive manner.

2. Customer Collaboration: "Another key principle of Agile is customer collaboration," Michael continued, his eyes lighting up with excitement. "Rather than working in isolation and relying on extensive documentation, Agile teams actively engage with customers throughout the project lifecycle to gather feedback, validate assumptions, and ensure alignment with customer needs and expectations."

He emphasized the importance of building strong relationships with stakeholders and fostering open communication channels to facilitate continuous collaboration and feedback.

3. Iterative Development: "Agile projects follow an iterative development approach, breaking down the project work into small, manageable chunks called iterations or sprints," Michael elaborated, sketching a series of overlapping circles on the whiteboard. "Each iteration focuses on delivering a specific set of features or functionality, allowing the team to iterate quickly, gather feedback, and adapt their approach based on the evolving requirements."

He encouraged the team to embrace the iterative mindset, emphasizing the value of incremental progress and continuous improvement in delivering value to the customer.

4. Self-Organizing Teams: "In Agile, teams are self-organizing and empowered to make decisions autonomously," Michael stated, his tone firm and resolute. "Rather than relying on hierarchical structures and micromanagement, Agile teams collaborate closely, share responsibilities, and collectively own the success of the project."

He urged the team to embrace their autonomy and accountability, empowering them to take ownership of their work and drive results collaboratively.

5. Continuous Improvement: "Finally, Agile emphasizes the importance of continuous improvement," Michael concluded, a smile playing on his lips. "By reflecting on their processes, seeking feedback, and experimenting with new approaches, Agile teams can adapt and evolve over time, becoming more effective and efficient with each iteration."

He challenged the team to embrace a culture of learning and experimentation, encouraging them to celebrate successes, learn from failures, and continuously strive for excellence in their Agile journey.

As the team absorbed Michael's insights and prepared to embark on their Agile project management adventure, a sense of excitement and anticipation filled the room. With their collective commitment to Agile principles and practices, they were ready to embrace change, collaborate with their customers, iterate quickly, self-organize effectively, and continuously improve their project outcomes.

Scrum Framework and Practices

As the sun dipped below the horizon, casting a warm glow over the city of Lusaka, Michael Carter gathered his team once again to delve into the intricacies of the Scrum framework and practices.

"Now that we understand the principles of Agile methodologies, let's explore one of the most popular frameworks used in Agile project management: Scrum," Michael began, his voice infused with a sense of excitement and anticipation. "Scrum provides a structured approach to Agile project management, with defined roles, ceremonies, and artifacts to guide the team through the iterative development process."

1. Roles in Scrum: "Our first step is to understand the various roles within the Scrum framework," Michael explained, gesturing to a diagram displayed on a nearby screen. "These include the Product Owner, who represents the voice of the customer and prioritizes the backlog; the Scrum Master, who facilitates the Scrum process and removes impediments; and the Development Team, who are responsible for delivering the increments of work."

He encouraged the team to embrace their respective roles and collaborate effectively to achieve the project goals.

2. Scrum Ceremonies: "Scrum defines several ceremonies or meetings to facilitate communication, collaboration, and decision-making within the team," Michael continued, flipping through a stack of colorful index cards. "These include the Sprint Planning meeting, where the team plans the work for the upcoming sprint; the Daily Standup, where team members share progress, challenges, and plans; the Sprint Review, where the team demonstrates the completed work to stakeholders; and the Sprint Retrospective, where the team reflects on their process and identifies opportunities for improvement."

He outlined the purpose and format of each ceremony, emphasizing the importance of active participation and engagement from all team members.

3. Product Backlog and Sprint Planning: "Central to the Scrum framework is the Product Backlog, a prioritized list of features, enhancements, and bug fixes that represent the work to be done," Michael explained, pointing to a digital backlog displayed on a collaborative board. "During Sprint Planning, the Product Owner and Development Team collaborate to select items from the Product Backlog and define the Sprint Goal, a short-term objective that guides the work for the upcoming sprint."

He encouraged the team to focus on delivering value to the customer by prioritizing high-value items and breaking them down into manageable tasks.

4. Sprint Execution and Daily Standup: "Once the Sprint Planning is complete, the team enters the Sprint Execution phase, where they work collaboratively to deliver the agreed-upon work," Michael said, his voice filled with energy and enthusiasm. "During the Daily Standup, team members gather for a brief, time-boxed meeting to share progress, discuss any impediments, and plan their activities for the day."

He stressed the importance of transparency, accountability, and communication during the sprint, enabling the team to adapt and respond to changing requirements quickly.

5. Sprint Review and Retrospective: "At the end of the sprint, the team holds a Sprint Review to demonstrate the completed work to stakeholders and gather feedback," Michael continued, his eyes gleaming with anticipation. "This feedback is used to inform future iterations and improve the product."

He emphasized the value of collaboration and customer engagement during the Sprint Review, enabling the team to validate assumptions and ensure alignment with stakeholder expectations.

6. Continuous Improvement: "Finally, Scrum encourages a culture of continuous improvement through the Sprint Retrospective," Michael concluded, a smile spreading across his face. "During this meeting, the team reflects on their process, identifies what went well and what could be improved, and commits to action items for the next sprint."

He challenged the team to embrace the spirit of experimentation and learning, empowering them to evolve and adapt their process iteratively.

As the team absorbed Michael's insights and prepared to embark on their Scrum journey, a sense of excitement and determination filled the room. With their collective commitment to the Scrum framework and practices, they were ready to embrace collaboration, transparency, and continuous improvement in their Agile project management endeavors.

Kanban System and Lean Project Management

As twilight descended upon the city of Lusaka, Michael Carter and his team gathered once more to explore the Kanban system and Lean project management principles.

"Now that we've covered Scrum, let's dive into another valuable Agile framework: Kanban, and the principles of Lean project management," Michael began, his voice resonating with enthusiasm and anticipation. "Kanban is a visual management method that helps teams improve workflow efficiency, reduce waste, and optimize processes."

1. Understanding the Kanban System: "Our first step is to understand the fundamentals of the Kanban system," Michael explained, gesturing toward a board adorned with colorful cards and columns. "Kanban visualizes the workflow using a board divided into columns representing different stages of the process. Tasks or user stories are represented by cards, which move across the board as work progresses."

He encouraged the team to embrace the principles of visual

management and transparency, enabling them to track work in progress and identify bottlenecks effectively.

2. Limiting Work in Progress (WIP): "A core principle of Kanban is limiting work in progress to maintain a smooth and steady flow of work," Michael continued, his eyes gleaming with intensity. "By setting WIP limits for each stage of the process, teams can prevent overloading and focus on completing tasks efficiently."

He emphasized the importance of respecting WIP limits and collaborating as a team to manage workload effectively, ensuring a balanced and sustainable pace of work.

3. Continuous Flow and Pull-Based Systems: "Kanban promotes a continuous flow of work and a pull-based system, where tasks are pulled into the workflow only when capacity allows," Michael explained, his gestures mirroring the fluidity of a flowing river. "This approach minimizes waste and maximizes value delivery by aligning work with actual demand."

He encouraged the team to embrace the principles of flow and pull, optimizing their processes to deliver value to the customer quickly and efficiently.

4. Lean Project Management Principles: "In addition to Kanban, we can draw insights from Lean project management principles to further enhance our Agile practices," Michael said, his voice infused with reverence for the timeless wisdom of Lean thinking. "Lean focuses on eliminating waste, optimizing resources, and maximizing value delivery to the customer."

He outlined key Lean principles such as value stream mapping, just-in-time production, and continuous improvement, encouraging the team to apply these principles to their project management practices.

5. Value Stream Mapping and Waste Elimination: "Value

stream mapping is a powerful Lean tool for identifying and eliminating waste in the project lifecycle," Michael explained, sketching a flowchart on a whiteboard. "By mapping out the entire process from start to finish, teams can identify bottlenecks, redundancies, and inefficiencies, and develop strategies to streamline the workflow."

He challenged the team to conduct value stream mapping exercises, uncovering opportunities for improvement and optimizing their project processes.

6. Continuous Improvement and Kaizen: "Finally, Lean project management encourages a culture of continuous improvement and Kaizen," Michael concluded, a smile spreading across his face. "By empowering teams to reflect on their processes, experiment with new approaches, and implement small, incremental changes, Lean enables organizations to evolve and thrive in a rapidly changing environment."

He urged the team to embrace the spirit of Kaizen, committing to ongoing learning and improvement in their Agile project management journey.

As the team absorbed Michael's insights and prepared to integrate Kanban and Lean principles into their Agile practices, a sense of excitement and determination filled the room. With their collective commitment to visual management, workflow optimization, and continuous improvement, they were ready to embark on a journey of Lean Agile excellence, delivering value to their customers with speed, efficiency, and precision.

Agile Roles and Responsibilities

As the twilight sky painted the city of Lusaka in hues of orange and purple, Michael Carter gathered his team once again to explore the roles and responsibilities in Agile project management.

"Now that we've covered various Agile frameworks and principles, let's delve into the roles and responsibilities that drive Agile success," Michael began, his voice carrying the weight of experience and knowledge. "In Agile, every team member plays a crucial role in delivering value to the customer and driving project success."

1. Product Owner: "Our first Agile role is that of the Product Owner," Michael explained, gesturing towards Sarah, a determined and focused member of the team. "The Product Owner is responsible for representing the voice of the customer, prioritizing the product backlog, and ensuring that the team delivers maximum value with each iteration."

He emphasized the importance of effective communication and collaboration between the Product Owner and the development team, enabling them to align their efforts with customer needs and expectations.

2. Scrum Master: "The Scrum Master serves as a servant-leader for the team, facilitating the Scrum process and removing impediments to progress," Michael continued, nodding towards John, a seasoned Scrum Master with a calm and reassuring demeanor. "They are responsible for coaching the team on Agile principles and practices, facilitating ceremonies, and fostering a culture of continuous improvement."

He highlighted the role of the Scrum Master in empowering the team to self-organize, collaborate effectively, and deliver high-quality results.

3. Development Team: "The Development Team consists of cross-functional members who collaborate to deliver increments of work," Michael said, casting his gaze across the room filled with diverse talents and skills. "They are responsible for planning, executing, and delivering the work agreed upon in each sprint, striving for excellence and continuous improvement."

He encouraged the team to embrace their collective accountability and ownership, leveraging their unique perspectives and expertise to deliver value to the customer.

4. Stakeholders: "Stakeholders play a vital role in Agile projects, providing feedback, guidance, and support throughout the project lifecycle," Michael continued, acknowledging the importance of external partners, customers, and sponsors. "Their involvement ensures alignment with organizational goals, validates assumptions, and helps prioritize work based on business value."

He emphasized the need for open and transparent communication with stakeholders, fostering trust and collaboration to drive project success.

5. Collaborative Culture: "In Agile, everyone is responsible for the success of the project," Michael concluded, a sense of conviction in his voice. "By fostering a collaborative culture, where individuals trust and support each other, Agile teams can overcome challenges, adapt to change, and deliver value to their customers with speed and efficiency."

He challenged the team to embrace their Agile roles and responsibilities fully, committing to collaboration, transparency, and continuous improvement in their project endeavors.

As the team absorbed Michael's insights and prepared to

embrace their Agile roles and responsibilities, a sense of unity and purpose filled the room. With their collective commitment to collaboration, empowerment, and accountability, they were ready to embark on their Agile journey, driving project success and delivering value to their customers with passion and dedication.

Iterative Development and Incremental Delivery

As the evening descended upon the bustling city of Lusaka, Michael Carter and his team gathered once more to explore the principles of iterative development and incremental delivery in Agile project management.

"Now that we've covered Agile roles and responsibilities, let's delve into the heart of Agile: iterative development and incremental delivery," Michael began, his voice resonating with confidence and conviction. "These principles lie at the core of Agile methodologies, enabling teams to adapt to change, deliver value early and often, and respond to customer feedback effectively."

1. Iterative Development: "Our first principle is iterative development, which involves breaking down the project into small, manageable increments or iterations," Michael explained, pacing back and forth with purpose. "Each iteration, or sprint, typically lasts two to four weeks and results in a potentially shippable product increment."

He emphasized the importance of embracing uncertainty and complexity, iterating rapidly to validate assumptions, learn from feedback, and deliver value incrementally.

2. Continuous Feedback Loop: "Central to iterative development is the continuous feedback loop, which enables teams to gather feedback early and often from stakeholders and end-users," Michael continued, his eyes gleaming with enthusiasm. "This feedback informs subsequent iterations, guiding the team in refining their product and ensuring alignment with customer needs and expectations."

He encouraged the team to prioritize customer collaboration, inviting feedback at every stage of the development process and adapting their plans accordingly.

3. Incremental Delivery: "In Agile, we aim to deliver value to the customer incrementally, with each iteration adding new features or enhancements to the product," Michael said, gesturing towards a whiteboard adorned with colorful sticky notes representing user stories. "By delivering increments of work regularly, we reduce the time to market, mitigate risk, and maximize the return on investment."

He highlighted the importance of prioritizing high-value features and releasing them to the customer early and often, enabling them to derive immediate benefits from the product.

4. Embracing Change: "One of the key tenets of Agile is embracing change," Michael continued, his voice filled with conviction. "By adopting an iterative approach to development, teams can respond to changing requirements, market conditions, and stakeholder feedback quickly and effectively."

He encouraged the team to remain flexible and adaptive, welcoming change as an opportunity for growth and improvement rather than a barrier to progress.

5. Adaptive Planning: "To support iterative development and incremental delivery, Agile teams practice adaptive planning, which involves continuously refining and adjusting their plans based on real-time feedback and insights," Michael explained, his words echoing the rhythm of the Agile manifesto.

"Rather than following a rigid plan, teams embrace uncertainty and complexity, adapting their approach to maximize value and minimize waste."

He challenged the team to embrace uncertainty and ambiguity, trusting in their ability to adapt and innovate in the face of change.

6. Continuous Improvement: "Finally, iterative development and incremental delivery embody the spirit of continuous improvement," Michael concluded, a smile spreading across his face. "By reflecting on their process, gathering feedback, and adapting their approach iteratively, Agile teams can deliver value to their customers with speed, efficiency, and precision."

He urged the team to embrace the principles of iterative development and incremental delivery fully, committing to continuous learning, adaptation, and improvement in their Agile journey.

As the team absorbed Michael's insights and prepared to embrace iterative development and incremental delivery in their Agile practices, a sense of excitement and determination filled the room. With their collective commitment to adaptability, collaboration, and continuous improvement, they were ready to embark on their Agile journey, delivering value to their customers with passion and purpose.

Measuring Success in Agile Projects

As the sun dipped below the horizon, casting a warm glow over the city of Lusaka, Michael Carter and his team gathered once more to explore the crucial aspect of measuring success in Agile projects.

"Now that we've discussed iterative development and incremental delivery, let's turn our attention to measuring success in Agile projects," Michael began, his voice steady and resolute. "In Agile, success is not just about delivering on time and within budget. It's about delivering value to the customer, fostering collaboration, and continuously improving the process."

1. Value Delivery Metrics: "Our first step in measuring success is to focus on value delivery metrics," Michael explained, his eyes scanning the room. "Rather than traditional metrics like budget variance or schedule adherence, Agile teams prioritize metrics that reflect the value delivered to the customer, such as business value delivered per iteration, customer satisfaction scores, and time to market."

He emphasized the importance of aligning metrics with organizational goals and customer expectations, ensuring that every action contributes to the overall success of the project.

2. Quality Metrics: "In Agile, quality is non-negotiable," Michael continued, his voice firm and unwavering. "To measure success, teams track quality metrics such as defect density, code churn, and customer-reported issues. By focusing on quality early and often, teams can prevent costly rework, maintain customer trust, and deliver a product that meets or exceeds expectations."

He challenged the team to prioritize quality at every stage of the development process, embracing practices such as test-driven development and continuous integration to ensure a high-quality end product.

3. Team Performance Metrics: "Another critical aspect of measuring success is assessing team performance," Michael said, his gaze resting on each team member in turn. "Agile teams track metrics such as velocity, cycle time, and sprint burndown to gauge their productivity, identify bottlenecks, and optimize their processes."

He encouraged the team to foster a culture of transparency and accountability, using performance metrics to drive continuous improvement and deliver value with speed and efficiency.

4. Stakeholder Satisfaction: "In Agile, the ultimate measure of success is stakeholder satisfaction," Michael continued, his voice filled with conviction. "Teams regularly solicit feedback from stakeholders and end-users, using surveys, interviews, and reviews to gauge satisfaction levels and identify areas for improvement."

He emphasized the importance of open and transparent communication with stakeholders, fostering trust and collaboration to ensure alignment with customer needs and expectations.

5. Adaptability and Flexibility: "Finally, in Agile, success is not just about hitting targets or achieving milestones," Michael concluded, a smile playing at the corners of his mouth. "It's about embracing adaptability and flexibility, responding to change, and continuously improving the process to deliver maximum value to the customer."

He urged the team to embrace uncertainty and ambiguity, trusting in their ability to adapt and innovate in the face of change, and to celebrate their successes, no matter how small, along the Agile journey.

6. Continuous Improvement: "As we strive for success in our Agile projects, let us commit to a culture of continuous improvement," Michael said, his words echoing the spirit of the Agile manifesto. "By reflecting on our process, gathering feedback, and adapting our approach iteratively, we can deliver value to our customers with speed, efficiency, and precision."

He challenged the team to embrace the principles of Agile fully, committing to collaboration, adaptability, and continuous improvement in their pursuit of success.

As the team absorbed Michael's insights and prepared to measure success in their Agile projects, a sense of determination and purpose filled the room. With their collective commitment to delivering value to their customers, fostering collaboration, and continuously improving their processes, they were ready to embark on their Agile journey with confidence and conviction.

5

Chapter 5: Effective Communication

Developing a Communication Plan

I n the heart of Lusaka, as the city buzzed with life, Michael Carter and his team gathered to delve into the intricacies of effective communication in project management.

"Welcome, everyone, to Chapter 5: Effective Communication," Michael announced, his voice carrying the weight of anticipation. "Today, we embark on a journey to understand the importance of clear, concise communication in driving project success."

1. Understanding Stakeholder Needs: "Our first step in effective communication is to understand the needs and expectations of our stakeholders," Michael explained, his gaze sweeping across the room. "By conducting stakeholder analysis and engagement assessments, we gain insights into their communication preferences, concerns, and desired frequency of updates."

He emphasized the importance of tailoring communication

strategies to meet the diverse needs of stakeholders, fostering trust and collaboration throughout the project lifecycle.

2. Defining Communication Objectives: "Once we understand our stakeholders, we can define clear communication objectives," Michael continued, his words resonating with purpose. "These objectives outline what information needs to be communicated, to whom, and when, ensuring that messages are relevant, timely, and aligned with project goals."

He encouraged the team to establish a communication plan that outlines key milestones, deliverables, and communication channels, facilitating effective coordination and collaboration among team members.

3. Selecting Communication Channels: "Effective communication relies on selecting the right channels to convey information," Michael said, his tone thoughtful. "Whether it's face-to-face meetings, emails, project management tools, or stakeholder portals, we must choose channels that are accessible, reliable, and conducive to clear communication."

He urged the team to leverage technology and tools to streamline communication processes, ensuring that information flows freely and transparently across the project team.

4. Establishing Feedback Mechanisms: "No communication plan is complete without feedback mechanisms," Michael continued, a spark of enthusiasm in his eyes. "By establishing regular feedback loops, we create opportunities for stakeholders to share their thoughts, concerns, and suggestions, enabling us to address issues promptly and adapt our communication strategies as needed."

He encouraged the team to embrace open and transparent communication, fostering a culture of collaboration and continuous improvement throughout the project lifecycle.

5. Managing Communication Risks: "In our journey towards effective communication, we must also be mindful of communication risks," Michael cautioned, his expression serious. "These may include misunderstandings, misinterpretations, or information overload, which can impede project progress and erode stakeholder trust."

He stressed the importance of proactively identifying and mitigating communication risks, fostering clarity and transparency in all project communications.

6. Monitoring and Adjusting: "Finally, effective communication requires ongoing monitoring and adjustment," Michael concluded, his voice filled with determination. "By regularly evaluating the effectiveness of our communication strategies and soliciting feedback from stakeholders, we can adapt our approach to ensure that information flows smoothly and accurately throughout the project lifecycle."

He challenged the team to embrace the principles of effective communication fully, committing to clarity, transparency, and collaboration in their project endeavors.

As the team absorbed Michael's insights and prepared to develop their communication plan, a sense of purpose and determination filled the room. With their collective commitment to effective communication, they were ready to navigate the complexities of project management with clarity, confidence, and collaboration.

Stakeholder Communication Strategies

In the vibrant city of Lusaka, Michael Carter and his team gathered once more to explore the intricacies of stakeholder communication strategies.

"Now that we've discussed the importance of clear communication, let's delve into stakeholder communication strategies," Michael began, his voice commanding attention. "Stakeholders play a crucial role in the success of any project, and effective communication is essential to keeping them informed, engaged, and satisfied."

1. Stakeholder Analysis: "Our first step in stakeholder communication is conducting a thorough stakeholder analysis," Michael explained, his tone earnest. "By identifying key stakeholders, understanding their interests, influence, and communication preferences, we can tailor our communication strategies to meet their needs effectively."

He urged the team to map out stakeholder relationships, prioritize their engagement, and anticipate their information needs throughout the project lifecycle.

2. Customized Communication Plans: "Once we've identified our stakeholders, we can develop customized communication plans for each group," Michael continued, his eyes alight with purpose. "These plans outline the frequency, format, and content of communication, ensuring that stakeholders receive timely and relevant information to support their involvement in the project."

He emphasized the importance of flexibility in communication plans, adapting them as stakeholder needs and project dynamics evolve over time.

3. Clear and Consistent Messaging: "In our communication with stakeholders, clarity and consistency are paramount," Michael said, his voice unwavering. "We must ensure that our messages are clear, concise, and free of jargon, enabling stakeholders to understand the project's objectives, progress, and challenges."

He encouraged the team to use a variety of communication channels, such as meetings, presentations, reports, and newsletters, to reach stakeholders effectively and reinforce key messages.

4. Engaging Stakeholders: "Effective communication goes beyond mere transmission of information; it's about engaging stakeholders in meaningful dialogue," Michael continued, his expression earnest. "We must create opportunities for stakeholders to provide feedback, ask questions, and participate in decision-making processes, fostering a sense of ownership and commitment to the project."

He challenged the team to cultivate a culture of openness and collaboration, inviting stakeholders to share their perspectives and contribute to project success.

5. Managing Expectations: "As we communicate with stakeholders, it's essential to manage their expectations effectively," Michael cautioned, his tone thoughtful. "We must be transparent about project goals, timelines, and potential risks, setting realistic expectations to avoid misunderstandings and dissatisfaction."

He stressed the importance of proactive communication, addressing stakeholder concerns promptly and openly to build trust and confidence in the project team.

6. Building Trust and Relationships: "Ultimately, stakeholder communication is about building trust and relationships," Michael concluded, a smile playing at the corners of his mouth. "By demonstrating transparency, accountability, and responsiveness in our communication, we can foster positive relationships with stakeholders and secure their support for the project."

He urged the team to prioritize stakeholder engagement

throughout the project lifecycle, recognizing the invaluable role that stakeholders play in project success.

As the team absorbed Michael's insights and prepared to implement stakeholder communication strategies, a sense of purpose and determination filled the room. With their collective commitment to engaging stakeholders effectively, they were ready to navigate the complexities of project management with clarity, confidence, and collaboration.

Managing Team Communication

In the bustling city of Lusaka, Michael Carter and his team reconvened to delve deeper into the realm of managing team communication.

"Now that we understand the importance of effective communication with stakeholders, let's explore managing team communication," Michael began, his voice commanding attention. "Clear and transparent communication within the project team is essential for fostering collaboration, ensuring alignment, and driving project success."

1. Establishing Communication Channels: "Our first step in managing team communication is establishing clear communication channels," Michael explained, his gaze sweeping across the room. "Whether it's team meetings, email, instant messaging, or project management tools, we must define how information flows within the team to ensure everyone is on the same page."

He emphasized the importance of selecting communication channels that are accessible, reliable, and conducive to collaboration, fostering transparency and accountability among team members.

2. Defining Communication Protocols: "Once we've established communication channels, we need to define communication protocols," Michael continued, his tone resolute. "These protocols outline when and how communication should occur, ensuring that team members know what information needs to be shared, to whom, and when."

He encouraged the team to establish norms for communication frequency, response times, and escalation procedures, fostering efficiency and clarity in team interactions.

3. Encouraging Open Dialogue: "In our project team, open dialogue and active listening are essential for effective communication," Michael said, his expression earnest. "We must create a culture where team members feel comfortable sharing their ideas, concerns, and feedback, fostering trust and collaboration."

He challenged the team to embrace diversity of thought and encourage constructive debate, recognizing that diverse perspectives lead to better decisions and innovative solutions.

4. Clarifying Roles and Responsibilities: "Clear communication also requires clarifying roles and responsibilities within the project team," Michael continued, his voice steady. "Each team member should understand their role, tasks, and expectations, ensuring accountability and alignment with project goals."

He urged the team to regularly revisit and clarify roles and responsibilities as the project evolves, adapting to changing priorities and dynamics to maintain clarity and focus.

5. Providing Timely Updates: "To keep the team informed and engaged, we must provide timely updates on project progress and developments," Michael said, his tone decisive. "Regular status meetings, progress reports, and informal check-ins enable team members to stay on track, address issues promptly, and celebrate achievements together."

He emphasized the importance of transparency in communication, sharing both successes and challenges openly to foster trust and collaboration within the team.

6. Resolving Conflicts Effectively: "Finally, effective communication also involves resolving conflicts and addressing issues promptly," Michael concluded, his voice filled with determination. "By fostering open dialogue and constructive problem-solving, we can address conflicts proactively, restore harmony, and maintain momentum towards project success."

He challenged the team to embrace conflict as an opportunity for growth, recognizing that healthy conflict resolution leads to stronger relationships and better outcomes.

As the team absorbed Michael's insights and prepared to implement effective team communication strategies, a sense of unity and purpose filled the room. With their collective commitment to clear and transparent communication, they were ready to collaborate seamlessly and navigate the complexities of project management with confidence and cohesion.

Tools for Effective Communication

In the heart of Lusaka, Michael Carter and his team gathered once more to explore the arsenal of tools available for effective communication within the project team.

"Now that we understand the principles of managing team communication, let's explore the tools that can help us facilitate clear and efficient communication," Michael began, his voice carrying a sense of anticipation. "Choosing the right communication tools is crucial for fostering collaboration, streamlining workflows, and keeping everyone aligned with project goals."

1. Project Management Software: "Our first tool for effective communication is project management software," Michael explained, his tone resolute. "Platforms like Asana, Trello, or Microsoft Project enable us to create tasks, assign responsibilities, and track progress in real-time, providing a centralized hub for collaboration and communication within the team."

He emphasized the importance of selecting a project management tool that aligns with the team's needs and preferences, facilitating seamless coordination and transparency throughout the project lifecycle.

2. Instant Messaging Platforms: "For quick and informal communication, instant messaging platforms are invaluable," Michael continued, his eyes alight with enthusiasm. "Tools like Slack, Microsoft Teams, or WhatsApp allow team members to exchange messages, share files, and collaborate in real-time, fostering spontaneous communication and rapid decision-making."

He encouraged the team to establish communication norms and etiquette for instant messaging, ensuring that it enhances rather than disrupts productivity and focus.

3. Video Conferencing Solutions: "In our increasingly remote and globalized world, video conferencing solutions play a vital role in connecting dispersed team members," Michael said, his expression thoughtful. "Platforms like Zoom, Google Meet, or Microsoft Teams enable us to conduct virtual meetings, workshops, and presentations, fostering face-to-face interaction and building rapport among team members."

He urged the team to leverage video conferencing for

regular team meetings, client presentations, and stakeholder engagement, bridging geographical barriers and enhancing collaboration.

4. Document Collaboration Tools: "For collaborative document editing and sharing, document collaboration tools are indispensable," Michael continued, his voice steady. "Platforms like Google Docs, Microsoft SharePoint, or Dropbox Paper enable team members to collaborate on documents in real-time, track changes, and provide feedback, facilitating seamless collaboration and version control."

He emphasized the importance of establishing document management protocols to ensure consistency, accuracy, and security in document collaboration processes.

5. Email and Newsletter Platforms: "Despite the rise of other communication tools, email remains a ubiquitous and indispensable tool for formal communication," Michael said, his tone pragmatic. "Platforms like Gmail, Outlook, or Mailchimp enable us to send formal announcements, updates, and newsletters to stakeholders, ensuring that important information reaches the right audience in a timely manner."

He encouraged the team to use email judiciously, balancing formal communication with other more interactive and collaborative channels.

6. Collaborative Whiteboarding Tools: "For brainstorming, visualizing ideas, and planning sessions, collaborative whiteboarding tools are invaluable," Michael concluded, his voice filled with conviction. "Platforms like Miro, Lucidchart, or Microsoft Whiteboard enable team members to sketch diagrams, map processes, and ideate together in real-time, fostering creativity and alignment."

He challenged the team to embrace visual collaboration tools as a means of enhancing creativity, engagement, and problem-solving within the team.

As the team absorbed Michael's insights and prepared to explore the array of communication tools available, a sense of excitement and possibility filled the room. With their collective commitment to leveraging technology for effective communication, they were ready to embrace innovation and collaboration in their project endeavors.

Conflict Resolution Techniques

In the bustling metropolis of Lusaka, Michael Carter and his team reconvened once more, this time to explore the delicate art of conflict resolution within the project team.

"Conflict is inevitable in any collaborative endeavor, but how we manage it can make all the difference," Michael began, his tone measured yet earnest. "Effective conflict resolution techniques are essential for maintaining harmony, fostering collaboration, and ensuring that team dynamics remain conducive to project success."

1. Active Listening: "Our first technique for resolving conflicts is active listening," Michael explained, his voice calm yet authoritative. "When conflicts arise, it's crucial to listen attentively to all parties involved, seeking to understand their perspectives, concerns, and underlying interests without judgment or interruption."

He urged the team to practice empathy and patience, acknowledging the emotions and perspectives of others while refraining from jumping to conclusions or making assumptions.

2. Constructive Dialogue: "Once we've listened to all

parties, we can engage in constructive dialogue to explore solutions collaboratively," Michael continued, his gaze steady. "By facilitating open and honest communication, we can encourage all parties to express their views, share their needs, and work together to find common ground."

He emphasized the importance of reframing conflicts as opportunities for growth and learning, fostering a culture of mutual respect and cooperation within the team.

3. Problem-Solving Approach: "Conflict resolution should be approached as a problem-solving exercise rather than a blame game," Michael asserted, his voice firm yet compassionate. "We must focus on addressing the underlying issues and finding mutually beneficial solutions that meet the needs of all parties involved."

He challenged the team to adopt a collaborative mindset, brainstorming creative solutions and considering the long-term implications of their decisions on project outcomes and team dynamics.

4. Mediation and Facilitation: "In situations where conflicts escalate or become entrenched, mediation and facilitation can help facilitate resolution," Michael suggested, his tone pragmatic. "A neutral third party, such as a project manager or HR representative, can help facilitate constructive dialogue, manage emotions, and guide the parties towards a mutually acceptable resolution."

He urged the team to seek assistance from trained mediators or facilitators when conflicts prove difficult to resolve internally, recognizing the value of impartiality and expertise in managing complex interpersonal dynamics.

5. Conflict De-escalation Techniques: "When conflicts escalate or become emotionally charged, it's essential to employ de-escalation techniques to diffuse tensions and restore calm," Michael continued, his voice steady. "Techniques such as taking a break, reframing the issue, or using humor can help defuse conflict, allowing all parties to regain perspective and approach the situation more rationally."

He encouraged the team to remain composed and empathetic in the face of conflict, recognizing that emotions play a significant role in interpersonal dynamics and conflict resolution.

6. Agreement and Follow-Up: "Once a resolution is reached, it's crucial to formalize the agreement and follow up to ensure that commitments are honored," Michael concluded, his expression earnest. "Documenting the agreed-upon solution, assigning responsibilities, and setting timelines for follow-up actions help reinforce accountability and prevent conflicts from recurring."

He challenged the team to embrace conflict resolution as an ongoing process, recognizing that conflicts may arise throughout the project lifecycle and require continual attention and effort to address effectively.

As the team absorbed Michael's insights and prepared to apply conflict resolution techniques in their project endeavors, a sense of empowerment and readiness filled the room. With their collective commitment to constructive dialogue and problem-solving, they were poised to navigate conflicts with grace, resilience, and collaboration, ensuring that interpersonal dynamics remained conducive to project success.

Reporting and Documentation

Michael Carter sat in the conference room, surrounded by the core members of his project team. They were nearing the end of their intensive training on effective communication, and today's focus was on the critical yet often overlooked aspect of reporting and documentation.

"Good communication isn't just about what we say in meetings or how we resolve conflicts," Michael began, his voice steady and clear. "It's also about how we document and report our progress, decisions, and challenges. Proper reporting and documentation ensure transparency, accountability, and continuity within the project."

1. Regular Status Reports: Michael turned to the whiteboard and wrote "Status Reports" in bold letters. "Regular status reports are essential for keeping everyone informed about the project's progress. These reports should include key updates, milestones achieved, upcoming tasks, and any issues or risks that need to be addressed."

He explained how each team member would be responsible for submitting their updates weekly, ensuring that all stakeholders had a clear understanding of where the project stood at any given moment.

2. Meeting Minutes: "Every meeting we hold should be documented with detailed minutes," Michael continued, turning to face the team. "Meeting minutes serve as an official record of the discussions, decisions, and action items agreed upon. They help us track progress, hold people accountable, and provide a reference point for future discussions."

He assigned rotating responsibilities for taking and distributing meeting minutes, emphasizing the importance of accuracy and timeliness in this process.

3. Decision Logs: "Keeping a decision log is crucial," Michael said, writing it on the board. "This document should capture all significant decisions made during the project, including the context, alternatives considered, and the rationale behind the final choice."

He stressed that a well-maintained decision log could help avoid revisiting past debates and ensure that everyone understood the reasoning behind critical project decisions.

4. Risk and Issue Logs: "Risk and issue logs are fundamental to proactive project management," Michael explained. "These logs should detail potential risks, their impact, likelihood, and the mitigation strategies we have in place. Similarly, issue logs should document any problems that arise, their status, and the steps being taken to resolve them."

Michael highlighted that these logs would be reviewed regularly during team meetings to ensure that risks and issues were being actively managed and addressed.

5. Communication Plans: "A comprehensive communication plan outlines how information will be disseminated throughout the project," Michael said. "It should specify the communication needs of all stakeholders, the methods and frequency of communication, and the responsible parties."

He encouraged the team to develop and adhere to this plan, ensuring that all stakeholders received timely and relevant updates in a consistent manner.

6. Project Documentation and Archiving: Finally, Michael addressed the importance of project documentation and archiving. "All project-related documents, including plans, reports, logs, and correspondence, should be systematically organized and archived. This practice ensures that we have a complete record of the project's history, which is invaluable for audits, lessons learned, and future projects."

He demonstrated the project's digital filing system, showing how documents should be categorized and stored for easy retrieval.

As the session concluded, Michael looked around the room, seeing a mix of determination and understanding in the eyes of his team members. "Remember, thorough reporting and documentation are not just bureaucratic tasks. They are the backbone of effective communication and project success. Let's commit to maintaining these standards and setting an example of excellence in project management."

With this final point, Michael knew they were equipped not just with the tools for effective communication, but with the mindset to prioritize and execute these practices diligently. Their journey toward project management excellence continued, fortified by a shared commitment to clarity, transparency, and accountability.

6

Chapter 6: Team Management and Leadership

Building a High-Performing Team

Michael Carter stood on the edge of the construction site, the sun rising behind him over the vast plains of Zambia. The project to provide clean water to the remote villages was not just a professional challenge but a personal mission. He knew that the key to the project's success was building a high-performing team.

As the morning mist began to lift, he gathered his team for their first official meeting. The group was a mix of local experts, international engineers, and volunteers, each bringing unique skills and perspectives.

"Good morning, everyone," Michael greeted, his voice carrying the weight of his responsibility. "We have a monumental task ahead of us, but I believe we can achieve great things together. Our first step is to become a cohesive, high-performing team."

1. Understanding Strengths and Weaknesses: Michael started with an icebreaker session where each member introduced themselves, sharing their backgrounds, strengths, and areas where they needed support. He emphasized the importance of knowing each other's capabilities to leverage their strengths and address any weaknesses collectively.

"By understanding where each of us excels and where we might need help, we can support one another and maximize our efficiency," Michael explained.

2. Clear Roles and Responsibilities: Next, Michael outlined the specific roles and responsibilities for each team member. He had spent the previous nights meticulously planning this, ensuring that everyone had a clear understanding of their tasks and how they fit into the larger project goals.

"Clear roles will help us avoid confusion and ensure that everyone knows what is expected of them," Michael said, pointing to the organizational chart he had pinned to a board. "Let's respect each other's roles and communicate openly if we face any challenges."

3. Setting Common Goals: Michael then led a discussion on the project's objectives, breaking down the long-term goals into manageable short-term milestones. He encouraged the team to voice their thoughts and collectively agree on the priorities.

"Our ultimate goal is to provide clean water, but we need to celebrate the small victories along the way," Michael stated. "Setting common goals will keep us aligned and motivated."

4. Encouraging Open Communication: He stressed the importance of open communication, creating an environment where team members felt safe to express their ideas, concerns, and feedback. Michael established regular check-ins and encouraged informal gatherings to build camaraderie.

"Communication is the lifeblood of our team," Michael asserted. "Whether it's a progress update or a concern about a potential issue, speak up. We're in this together."

5. Building Trust and Respect: Michael knew that trust and respect were fundamental to any high-performing team. He led by example, showing respect for each team member's expertise and making it clear that he valued their contributions.

"Trust is earned through respect and reliability," Michael said. "Let's build that trust by being dependable and showing respect for each other's work and opinions."

6. Providing Support and Resources: Lastly, Michael committed to providing the necessary support and resources. He assured the team that he would advocate for their needs, whether it was additional training, equipment, or manpower.

"If you need something to do your job well, come to me," Michael promised. "I'm here to support you, and together, we will overcome any obstacle."

As the meeting concluded, Michael felt a sense of optimism. The team dispersed to their tasks, energized by the clear direction and newfound sense of unity. He watched them go, knowing that the foundation of a high-performing team was being laid brick by brick.

With this strong start, Michael believed they could turn their collective vision into reality. The journey would be challenging, but with a high-performing team, nothing seemed insurmountable.

Roles and Responsibilities within a Project Team

The sun was high in the sky when Michael called for a second meeting in the communal tent that served as their project office. The team, a diverse group of engineers, technicians, local workers, and volunteers, gathered with a palpable mix of curiosity and anticipation.

"Alright, everyone, let's dive into our roles and responsibilities," Michael began, his voice steady and confident. He unfurled a large sheet of paper pinned to a board, revealing a detailed organizational chart.

1. Project Manager: Michael Carter "First up, the Project Manager. That's me," Michael said with a slight smile. "My job is to oversee the entire project, ensure we're meeting our goals, and troubleshoot any issues that arise. I'll also be your primary point of contact with our stakeholders and sponsors."

He paused to let that sink in, then continued, "But remember, I can't do this alone. Each of you plays a crucial role in our success."

2. Lead Engineer: David Mbete "David Mbete, you're our Lead Engineer," Michael announced, nodding towards a tall, bespectacled man with a calm demeanor. "You'll be responsible for all engineering aspects of the project. This includes designing the water systems, overseeing the construction, and ensuring everything meets our safety standards."

David gave a nod of acknowledgment, his face serious but determined.

3. Operations Manager: Sarah Johnson "Sarah Johnson, you'll be our Operations Manager," Michael continued, turning to a woman with a no-nonsense attitude. "You'll manage the day-to-day logistics, coordinate supplies, and ensure we stay on schedule."

Sarah gave a brisk nod, already scribbling notes in her planner.

4. Community Liaison: Bwalya Ngoma "Bwalya Ngoma, our Community Liaison," Michael said, addressing a young man who had grown up in the nearby village. "Your role is critical. You'll work closely with the local communities, ensuring their needs and concerns are addressed and helping us integrate our efforts with local initiatives."

Bwalya smiled warmly, his connection to the community evident in his enthusiastic nod.

5. Environmental Specialist: Dr. Anita Patel "Dr. Anita Patel, you're our Environmental Specialist," Michael announced, looking at a woman with a keen interest in sustainable practices. "Your job is to make sure our project is environmentally sustainable. You'll conduct impact assessments and ensure we're compliant with environmental regulations."

Dr. Patel gave a thoughtful nod, already considering the environmental challenges ahead.

6. Volunteer Coordinator: Tom Reynolds "Tom Reynolds, our Volunteer Coordinator," Michael said, pointing to a young man with an easygoing demeanor. "You'll manage our volunteers, making sure they have what they need to be effective and safe. You'll also organize training sessions and ensure everyone is aligned with our goals."

Tom flashed a thumbs-up, his enthusiasm clear to everyone in the room.

Defining the Roles Clearly: Michael took a moment to look around the room, ensuring everyone was following. "Defining these roles clearly helps us avoid overlap and confusion," he explained. "It also ensures that each of you knows exactly what is expected and who to turn to for specific issues."

Establishing Accountability: "Accountability is key," Michael continued. "We need to trust each other to handle our respective areas. If you encounter a problem, don't hesitate to bring it up. We're a team, and we'll solve these issues together."

Encouraging Collaboration: "While we have defined roles, collaboration is essential," Michael emphasized. "We will need to work together, share insights, and support one another. The success of one area is tied to the success of the whole project."

Regular Check-ins and Communication: Michael then highlighted the importance of regular check-ins. "We'll have daily briefings to ensure everyone is on track and address any emerging issues. Open communication will keep us aligned and help us adapt swiftly to any changes."

Final Thoughts: As the meeting wrapped up, Michael looked around the room once more, feeling a surge of optimism. "Remember, each role is vital. Let's respect each other's responsibilities and work together towards our common goal. This is how we turn our workforce into a winforce."

The team dispersed, each member more aware of their critical role in the project. Michael watched them go, his confidence bolstered by their professionalism and commitment. They were ready to tackle the challenges ahead, united by clear roles and a shared vision.

Motivating and Engaging Team Members

Michael stood at the edge of the project site, watching the team as they worked under the scorching Zambian sun. The initial energy and excitement of the project's launch had begun to wane, and he could sense the fatigue setting in. It was time to reinvigorate the team.

That evening, Michael called for an impromptu meeting around a bonfire. The flames flickered against the darkening sky, casting a warm glow on the team's faces. As everyone gathered, Michael could see the weariness in their eyes, but he also saw the determination that had brought them this far.

"Thank you all for coming," Michael began, his voice carrying a mix of gratitude and resolve. "I know it's been tough, and the days are long. But tonight, I want to remind us why we're here and how we can support each other through the challenges."

1. Sharing the Vision: "Let's start with why we're doing this," Michael continued. He pulled out a photo of the local children playing by the river, where clean water was a scarce luxury. "This is who we're working for. Our project isn't just about building a water system; it's about transforming lives. Every pipe we lay, every trench we dig brings us closer to giving these children a healthier future."

The team looked at the photo, the reminder of their mission rekindling a spark of motivation. Michael could see shoulders straighten and eyes brighten with renewed purpose.

2. Celebrating Small Wins: "We've already made significant progress," Michael said, turning the focus to their achievements. "The foundations are laid, and the community is already seeing the benefits. Tonight, let's take a moment to celebrate our small wins."

He handed out slips of paper, asking each team member to write down a recent achievement or positive moment. They then shared these aloud, from overcoming a challenging technical issue to the community's warm reception. The air filled with applause and laughter, the simple act of recognition lifting spirits.

3. Providing Support and Encouragement: "Next, I want to talk about support," Michael said, his tone serious but encouraging. "We all have tough days. If you see a colleague struggling, offer a hand or an encouraging word. We're a team, and we need to lift each other up."

David Mbete, the Lead Engineer, spoke up. "I remember when we hit that bedrock last week, and it seemed impossible to break through. But with everyone's help, we did it. We can get through anything together."

Nods of agreement rippled through the group, the reminder of their collective strength boosting morale.

4. Ensuring Opportunities for Growth: "Let's also focus on growth," Michael added. "This project is a learning opportunity for all of us. If there's something you're interested in or a skill you want to develop, let me know. We'll find ways to make it happen."

Sarah Johnson, the Operations Manager, chimed in. "I'm organizing a few workshops on project management software. It's a great chance to learn something new and improve our efficiency."

5. Fostering a Positive Work Environment: "Creating a positive work environment is crucial," Michael emphasized. "Let's keep this space respectful, inclusive, and supportive. If anyone has concerns or ideas to improve our work conditions, speak up."

Bwalya Ngoma, the Community Liaison, raised his hand. "I think we could use some more team-building activities. Maybe a weekly soccer game with the locals?"

Laughter and enthusiastic agreement followed, the idea of mixing work with play appealing to everyone.

6. Leading by Example: Finally, Michael looked around at his team, his expression earnest. "I promise to lead by example. I'll be here with you in the trenches, facing the same challenges. Together, we'll push through the hard times and celebrate the successes."

The team dispersed, their spirits visibly lifted. Michael felt a sense of satisfaction as he watched them go, chatting and laughing with each other. He knew the road ahead would still be tough, but tonight had reminded them all why they were here and how powerful they could be when united.

As the fire burned low, Michael stayed behind for a moment, gazing into the flames. The flickering light symbolized the potential and resilience of his team. With renewed energy and a clear vision, they were ready to tackle whatever challenges lay ahead, turning their workforce into a true winforce.

Delegation and Empowerment

Michael stood before a whiteboard in the makeshift project office, the clatter of construction work echoing outside. The team gathered around him, curious about the meeting's agenda. They had just completed a major phase of the water project, and Michael knew it was time to reassign tasks and responsibilities.

"Good morning, everyone," Michael began, his tone upbeat. "We've done an incredible job so far, and now we need to ensure we maintain this momentum. Today, we're going to talk about delegation and empowerment."

1. The Importance of Delegation: He picked up a marker and wrote "Delegation" at the top of the whiteboard. "Delegation isn't just about handing off tasks," he explained. "It's about trust and empowering each of you to take ownership.

This project is too big for any one person to handle alone, and that's why we need to distribute responsibilities effectively."

Michael paused, looking at each team member. "By delegating, we ensure that no one is overwhelmed, and everyone has the chance to contribute their best."

2. Assigning Tasks Based on Strengths: Michael turned to the whiteboard, writing down key tasks that needed attention: procurement, logistics, community engagement, technical oversight, and safety management.

"David," he said, looking at the Lead Engineer, "you've got a knack for technical challenges. I want you to oversee the installation of the new filtration systems. Sarah, you're great with details and organization, so I'm assigning you to manage procurement and logistics. Bwalya, your connection with the community is invaluable. You'll continue to lead community engagement."

He continued, matching tasks with individuals based on their strengths and expertise. The team members nodded, some with renewed confidence, others with a hint of nervousness at the increased responsibility.

3. Providing Clear Instructions and Expectations: "Clear instructions and expectations are crucial," Michael continued. "I'm here to support you, but I also trust each of you to take these tasks and run with them. Let's be clear about deadlines and deliverables. If you need help or resources, speak up."

He handed out detailed briefs for each assigned task, ensuring everyone understood their new roles and responsibilities.

4. Encouraging Autonomy: Michael took a step back, giving the team room to digest their new assignments. "I encourage autonomy," he said. "Feel free to make decisions within your domain. You don't need to come to me for every small thing. Use your judgment, and trust your instincts."

Sarah spoke up. "So, if I find a local supplier who can deliver materials faster, I can go ahead and place the order?"

"Exactly," Michael replied with a smile. "You're in charge of procurement now. Make the call."

5. Providing Support and Resources: Michael knew that empowerment also meant providing the necessary support. "If you run into any obstacles, I'm here to help. We're all here to support each other. Let's set up regular check-ins to discuss progress and address any issues."

He arranged for weekly meetings where the team could share updates, seek advice, and collaborate on solutions. This open line of communication would ensure everyone felt supported and connected.

6. Recognizing and Celebrating Initiative: "Finally," Michael said, "I want to recognize and celebrate your initiative. When you take ownership and make things happen, it deserves acknowledgment."

He announced a new initiative: a "Project Star" award for team members who showed exceptional leadership and initiative. This would not only motivate the team but also highlight the importance of taking charge and making impactful decisions.

As the meeting wrapped up, Michael felt a sense of accomplishment. He had seen the initial flicker of empowerment in his team's eyes, a sign that they were ready to take on their new responsibilities with confidence.

David approached him after the meeting, a determined look on his face. "Thanks, Michael. I appreciate the trust. I'm looking forward to tackling this new challenge."

"You've got this, David," Michael replied, clapping him on the shoulder. "And remember, we're all in this together."

Walking out of the office, Michael watched his team disperse, each member now armed with a renewed sense of purpose and ownership. He knew that by empowering his team, he had not only lightened his own load but also unleashed the full potential of each team member. The project's success would now be a shared achievement, built on the foundation of trust and collaboration.

Managing Remote and Distributed Teams

Michael sat in his modest project office, a laptop open before him. The room was a hive of activity, with team members bustling about, but Michael's focus was on the screen. He had a crucial virtual meeting with team members scattered across Zambia and beyond. The water project had expanded, requiring expertise from remote specialists and distributed teams.

As the meeting commenced, familiar faces appeared in the video windows—some from Lusaka, others from remote villages, and even a couple of international consultants. Michael greeted everyone with a warm smile, appreciating the diverse array of talent before him.

"Good afternoon, everyone," Michael began, his voice steady and welcoming. "Thank you all for joining. Today, we're going to discuss how we can effectively manage our remote and distributed teams to ensure we remain cohesive and productive."

1. Establishing Clear Communication Channels: Michael shared his screen, displaying a communication matrix he had developed. "First, we need clear communication channels," he explained. "Email for official documentation, Slack for quick questions and updates, and Zoom for our regular face-to-face meetings."

He highlighted the importance of regular check-ins and maintaining a structured communication schedule to keep everyone aligned, regardless of their physical location.

2. Setting Expectations and Deliverables: "Next, let's talk about expectations," Michael continued. "We need clear deliverables and deadlines. Each team should know what's expected and by when."

He outlined specific tasks and assigned deadlines, ensuring each remote team member knew their role in the project. "John, you're overseeing the supply chain from Lusaka. Anna, you'll handle the community outreach in the northern villages. Let's make sure we stick to our timelines and report any delays immediately."

3. Building Trust and Team Cohesion: Michael knew that trust was crucial, especially with a dispersed team. "Trust is key," he said. "We need to trust each other to get the job done, even if we're miles apart."

He proposed virtual team-building activities and regular updates to build camaraderie. "Let's share our successes and challenges. A weekly highlight reel can keep us connected and motivated."

4. Leveraging Technology and Tools: "Technology is our friend here," Michael stated. "Let's use project management tools like Trello and Asana to track our progress. These platforms will help us stay organized and transparent."

He demonstrated how to use these tools, showing how tasks could be assigned, tracked, and completed efficiently. The team members nodded, appreciating the structured approach.

5. Handling Time Zone Differences: With team members in different time zones, coordination was a challenge. Michael addressed this with sensitivity. "We're spread across different time zones, so let's be mindful of each other's schedules."

He proposed a rotating meeting schedule to accommodate everyone and set core hours for real-time collaboration. "Let's use asynchronous communication where possible. Record meetings and share minutes so everyone stays informed, even if they can't attend live."

6. Encouraging Feedback and Continuous Improvement: "Finally, feedback is essential," Michael concluded. "Let's keep improving our processes. If something isn't working, speak up."

He encouraged an open feedback loop, where team members could share their experiences and suggest improvements. "Your input is invaluable," he said. "Together, we can refine our approach and ensure this project's success."

As the meeting drew to a close, Michael felt a sense of accomplishment. Managing a remote and distributed team was challenging, but he was confident that with clear communication, trust, and the right tools, they could overcome any obstacles.

After the meeting, Michael received an email from John in Lusaka. "Michael, thanks for the detailed plan and clear expectations. I feel much more connected to the team now, even from afar."

Michael smiled, responding with encouragement. "Glad to hear that, John. Let's keep the momentum going."

He leaned back in his chair, looking out at the bustling project site. Despite the distance, his team was united in their mission, working together to bring clean water to Zambia. The project's success would be a testament to their collective effort and the power of effective remote team management.

Leadership Styles and Their Impact on Projects

Michael stood before his team, his mind racing through the different leadership styles he had studied over the years. He knew that the success of their water project in Zambia hinged not just on their collective skills and resources, but also on his ability to lead effectively. The team was diverse, with members from various cultural backgrounds and professional experiences, and it was clear that a one-size-fits-all leadership approach wouldn't suffice.

1. Transformational Leadership: Michael decided to start with transformational leadership. "Team, let's aim high," he said, his voice filled with enthusiasm. "I believe in inspiring and motivating each of you to reach your full potential. Together, we can make a significant impact on this community."

His passion was contagious, and he saw the team's eyes light up with a renewed sense of purpose. Transformational leadership, he realized, was about creating a vision that everyone could rally behind.

2. Transactional Leadership: But Michael also knew that structure and discipline were necessary. "Alongside our vision, we need clear goals and rewards," he continued. "I'll be implementing a system where exceptional work is recognized and rewarded. Meeting our milestones on time will earn you tangible rewards."

The promise of recognition and rewards for hard work kept the team focused and driven. Michael saw this transactional leadership style as a way to maintain high performance and accountability.

3. Servant Leadership: Michael then switched gears to servant leadership. "I want you to know that I am here to support you in any way I can," he said earnestly. "Your needs come first. If there are obstacles in your way, it's my job to help remove them."

By putting his team first, Michael fostered an environment of trust and cooperation. The team felt valued and supported, knowing their leader was genuinely invested in their well-being.

4. Autocratic Leadership: However, Michael also understood that certain situations demanded a more directive approach. "In critical moments, I might need to make quick, decisive calls," he explained. "During crises, we'll need to act swiftly and follow a clear, unambiguous direction."

While the team appreciated Michael's inclusive approach, they also respected his ability to take charge when needed. This autocratic leadership style ensured that they could navigate urgent situations efficiently.

5. Democratic Leadership: Michael valued the input of his team and believed in the power of collaborative decision-making. "Your opinions matter," he said. "We'll have regular meetings where everyone can voice their ideas and concerns. Decisions will be made collectively."

The democratic leadership style empowered the team, making them feel integral to the project's success. Michael noticed an increase in creativity and innovation as team members felt more comfortable sharing their ideas.

6. Laissez-Faire Leadership: Finally, Michael acknowledged the importance of giving his team the freedom to operate independently. "I trust each of you to manage your tasks," he said. "You have the expertise, and I'll step back to let you shine."

This laissez-faire approach allowed the team to take ownership of their work, fostering a sense of autonomy and responsibility. Michael found that this balance of freedom and support led to a highly motivated and self-reliant team.

Michael concluded the meeting with a reflective note. "Leadership isn't about sticking to one style," he said. "It's about adapting to the needs of the project and the team. By combining these different approaches, we can achieve our goals and make a real difference."

As he stepped down from the makeshift podium, Michael felt a deep sense of satisfaction. His team was ready, motivated, and united under a versatile and dynamic leadership approach. The road ahead was challenging, but with the right leadership, he was confident they could navigate any obstacle and achieve their mission.

Chapter 7: Risk Management

Identifying Potential Risks

T he early morning sun cast long shadows over the bustling camp. Michael stood at the edge of the project site, surveying the progress. The water project was advancing steadily, but he knew they had to remain vigilant. Risk management was crucial, especially in a challenging environment like Zambia.

Michael gathered his core team in the central tent. Maps, charts, and laptops cluttered the large table. "Today, we're focusing on risk management," he began. "Identifying potential risks early is vital to our project's success."

1. Environmental Risks: "Let's start with environmental risks," Michael said, pointing to a large map of the region. "We need to consider weather patterns, potential floods, and droughts. The rainy season is approaching, and it could impact our work."

Anna, the environmental specialist, added, "We should also

monitor for possible contamination of water sources. Any changes in water quality can derail our progress and harm the local communities."

2. Resource Risks: Michael turned to John, the logistics manager. "John, what about our resources?"

John nodded, "Supply chain disruptions are a real threat. We need to ensure we have backup suppliers for critical materials and keep an eye on fuel availability for our machinery."

3. Technical Risks: "Technical failures are another major concern," Michael continued. "Equipment breakdowns, software glitches in our project management tools, or issues with the new water filtration system could cause delays."

Natasha, the technical lead, suggested, "Regular maintenance schedules and having spare parts on hand will mitigate some of these risks. Also, training the team to handle minor technical issues can help keep things running smoothly."

4. Human Risks: "The human factor can't be overlooked," Michael said, looking around the table. "Team health and safety, potential conflicts, and even turnover can affect our project."

Dr. Mwansa, the team doctor, emphasized, "We need strict health protocols, especially with the ongoing malaria risk. Providing proper PPE and ensuring a safe working environment is essential."

5. Political and Social Risks: "Lastly, political and social factors," Michael stated. "Changes in local government policies, community resistance, or social unrest can create significant hurdles."

Anna chimed in again, "Building strong relationships with local leaders and the community will help us navigate these challenges. Regular engagement and transparency are key."

6. Financial Risks: Michael concluded with financial risks. "Funding is always a concern. Any delays or cost overruns can strain our budget."

The financial advisor, Peter, reassured the team, "We'll keep a close eye on expenditures and maintain a contingency fund to cover unexpected costs. Regular financial reviews will keep us on track."

With a comprehensive list of potential risks laid out, Michael felt more prepared. "Great work, team," he said, wrapping up the session. "We'll create detailed risk management plans for each category and review them regularly. Our proactive approach will be our strongest defense against these challenges."

As the team dispersed, Michael felt a sense of relief. Identifying potential risks was just the first step, but it was a crucial one. With a vigilant eye and a well-prepared team, he was confident they could mitigate these risks and keep the project on course, ensuring clean water for the people of Zambia.

Qualitative and Quantitative Risk Analysis

The morning air in the camp was buzzing with a mix of anticipation and urgency. Michael knew that identifying potential risks was only the beginning. The next crucial step was to analyze these risks both qualitatively and quantitatively to prioritize their management.

In the main tent, the core team gathered once more around the large table, now filled with charts, graphs, and laptops. Michael began the meeting with a sense of determined focus. "Today, we're diving into risk analysis. We need to assess and prioritize these risks using both qualitative and quantitative methods."

1. Qualitative Risk Analysis:

"Let's start with qualitative analysis," Michael said, handing out risk assessment sheets. "We'll evaluate the impact and likelihood of each risk using a simple scale from low to high."

The team began their work, discussing each risk identified in their previous meeting.

Anna spoke first. "For environmental risks, such as potential flooding, I'd rate the impact as high and the likelihood as medium."

Michael nodded. "Agreed. What about technical risks, Natasha?"

Natasha responded thoughtfully, "Equipment breakdowns could have a high impact but a low likelihood if we stick to our maintenance schedule."

As the team continued, they color-coded risks based on their assessments. Red for high impact and high likelihood, yellow for medium, and green for low. The visual representation helped them quickly see which risks required immediate attention.

2. Quantitative Risk Analysis:

Next, Michael shifted the focus to quantitative analysis. "Now, let's look at the numbers. We need to quantify the potential impact of these risks in terms of time, cost, and resources."

Peter, the financial advisor, took the lead. "We'll use Expected Monetary Value (EMV) calculations. For example, if the likelihood of equipment failure is 10% and the potential cost is $50,000, the EMV is $5,000."

Michael watched as the team calculated EMVs for various risks. "This helps us allocate our contingency budget more effectively," he noted.

John, the logistics manager, highlighted another example. "If delays due to supply chain disruptions have a 20% likelihood with a potential cost of $100,000, the EMV is $20,000."

Michael emphasized the importance of these calculations. "Quantifying risks allows us to prioritize them based on their potential financial impact, ensuring we allocate resources where they're most needed."

3. Risk Probability and Impact Matrix:

To further refine their analysis, the team created a risk probability and impact matrix. This tool visually mapped the risks based on their qualitative and quantitative assessments, providing a clear picture of their priorities.

4. Sensitivity Analysis:

Michael introduced sensitivity analysis to understand how variations in key assumptions affected risk outcomes. "Let's see how changes in likelihood or impact influence our risk exposure," he suggested.

Natasha ran scenarios through the project management software, demonstrating how even small changes in assumptions could significantly alter their risk profile. This analysis helped the team understand which risks were most sensitive to change and required closer monitoring.

5. Simulation Techniques:

Peter proposed using simulation techniques, like Monte Carlo simulations, to model risk scenarios. "By simulating various outcomes, we can see a range of potential impacts and better prepare for uncertainties."

The team watched as Peter ran simulations, producing a range of possible project outcomes. This provided a probabilistic view of risks, helping them anticipate potential challenges more accurately.

6. Decision Trees:

Finally, Michael introduced decision trees to analyze risks with multiple possible outcomes. "Decision trees help us visualize different paths and make informed decisions based on their potential consequences."

Anna presented a decision tree for environmental risks, showing various outcomes based on different mitigation strategies. This tool helped the team evaluate their options and choose the best course of action.

With both qualitative and quantitative analyses complete, Michael felt more confident in their risk management strategy. "Excellent work, everyone. We've now identified, analyzed, and prioritized our risks. This comprehensive approach will guide us in effectively managing these challenges as we move forward."

As the team dispersed to implement their plans, Michael took a moment to reflect. The risks were real and varied, but with thorough analysis and a well-prepared team, they were equipped to handle whatever came their way. The success of their water project in Zambia depended on it.

Developing Risk Response Strategies

Michael stood before the whiteboard in the main tent, the risk matrix and EMV charts pinned up beside him. The team had identified and analyzed the risks; now, it was time to develop strategies to manage them effectively. The hum of generators and distant sounds of construction provided a backdrop as they prepared for this critical phase of planning.

"Alright, team," Michael began, "we need to turn our analysis into action. Our goal is to develop comprehensive response strategies for each major risk. Let's start with the environmental risks."

1. Avoidance Strategies:

Anna, the environmental specialist, was first to speak. "For the potential flooding risk, I suggest we avoid building in low-lying areas prone to flooding. We could also create barriers and drainage systems to redirect water flow away from our construction sites."

Michael nodded, writing 'Avoid' on the whiteboard under the flooding risk. "Good. Avoidance can significantly reduce our exposure. Now, let's consider the risk of equipment failure."

2. Mitigation Strategies:

Natasha, the technical lead, chimed in. "For equipment breakdowns, we can mitigate this risk by setting up a rigorous maintenance schedule and having backup equipment on standby. Additionally, training local technicians to handle repairs can reduce downtime."

Michael added 'Mitigate' next to equipment failure and detailed Natasha's suggestions. "Perfect. Mitigation will help minimize the impact if the risk does materialize. What about our supply chain disruptions?"

3. Transfer Strategies:

John, the logistics manager, suggested, "We can transfer some of the risk by negotiating contracts with suppliers that include penalties for delays. This not only incentivizes timely deliveries but also provides us with compensation to cover any additional costs if delays occur."

"Good thinking," Michael said, writing 'Transfer' on the board. "Transferring risk can help us manage our exposure by sharing it with other parties. Now, how about the risk of political instability?"

4. Acceptance Strategies:

Peter, the financial advisor, offered a realistic perspective. "Given the nature of the region, we might have to accept some level of political risk. We can't control it, but we can prepare contingency plans and set aside emergency funds to manage the consequences."

Michael wrote 'Accept' next to political instability and nodded thoughtfully. "Sometimes acceptance is the best we can do, especially when the risk is beyond our control. We must be prepared for rapid response and adaptation."

5. Contingency Planning:

Michael continued, "For all these strategies, we need detailed contingency plans. For instance, if flooding occurs despite our avoidance strategies, we should have evacuation plans and alternative work sites ready."

Anna added, "We could also create flood response teams and train them to act quickly in an emergency."

"Excellent," Michael replied, noting the suggestions. "Let's also discuss our contingency plans for equipment failure. Natasha, can you outline a quick response protocol?"

6. Implementation and Monitoring:

Natasha agreed. "We should have a system for immediate reporting of equipment issues, rapid dispatch of repair teams, and a checklist to follow for each type of equipment failure."

Michael emphasized the importance of monitoring. "We'll need a robust monitoring system to track these risks continuously. Regularly updating our risk assessments and response strategies based on new information is crucial."

As the meeting concluded, Michael felt a renewed sense of confidence. The team had crafted a solid framework for managing risks, transforming potential threats into manageable challenges.

"We've got our strategies in place," Michael said, looking around the table. "Now, let's ensure everyone knows their roles and responsibilities in these plans. Our success depends on our preparation and our ability to adapt swiftly to any situation."

The team dispersed to their respective tasks, each carrying a piece of the risk management puzzle. Michael knew that the path ahead was fraught with uncertainty, but with their well-laid plans, they were equipped to face whatever came their way. The success of the water project—and the well-being of countless Zambian communities—depended on it.

Implementing Risk Mitigation Plans

In the heart of the camp, the project team gathered around a makeshift table strewn with maps, schedules, and communication devices. Michael stood at the head, a sense of urgency in his demeanor as they delved into the next phase of their risk management strategy: implementation.

"Alright, everyone," Michael began, his voice cutting through the ambient sounds of the camp. "We've developed our risk mitigation plans. Now it's time to put them into action."

1. Mobilizing Resources:

Anna, the environmental specialist, spoke first. "For our flood mitigation plan, we need to mobilize resources to construct barriers and drainage systems. We also need to ensure we have the necessary equipment and manpower ready."

John, the logistics manager, nodded in agreement. "I'll coordinate with our suppliers to expedite the delivery of materials and equipment needed for the flood defenses. We can't afford any delays."

2. Training and Preparedness:

Natasha, the technical lead, chimed in. "To implement our equipment maintenance plan effectively, we need to ensure our technicians are trained and equipped to handle repairs. We'll conduct training sessions and simulate equipment breakdown scenarios to test our response readiness."

Michael nodded, impressed with the proactive approach. "Good. Training and preparedness are key to minimizing downtime and maintaining project momentum."

3. Establishing Communication Channels:

Peter, the financial advisor, added, "We need robust communication channels to ensure everyone is informed and can act swiftly in case of any unforeseen events. Regular updates and clear protocols will be essential."

Michael agreed. "Communication is vital. Let's establish dedicated channels for reporting and escalating risks, as well as for disseminating updates and changes to our mitigation plans."

4. Monitoring and Evaluation:

As the team discussed their plans, Michael emphasized the importance of continuous monitoring and evaluation. "We can't just set these plans in motion and forget about them. We need to constantly monitor their effectiveness and adjust as necessary."

Anna nodded. "Exactly. Regular inspections of our flood defenses, equipment maintenance logs, and feedback from on-the-ground teams will provide valuable insights into the success of our mitigation efforts."

5. Flexibility and Adaptation:

Natasha added, "We also need to remain flexible and adaptable. Despite our best efforts, unforeseen challenges may arise. We must be prepared to adjust our plans accordingly."

Michael nodded in agreement. "Agreed. Flexibility is key. We need to have contingency plans in place for any potential deviations from our initial strategies."

6. Stakeholder Engagement:

Before concluding the meeting, Michael addressed the importance of stakeholder engagement in implementing their risk mitigation plans. "We need to keep our stakeholders informed and involved every step of the way. Their support and cooperation are crucial to our success."

As the meeting drew to a close, the team dispersed, each member tasked with specific responsibilities to execute their risk mitigation plans. Michael watched them go, a sense of determination burning bright within him. The road ahead was fraught with challenges, but with their meticulous planning and proactive approach to risk management, they were well-prepared to overcome whatever obstacles lay in their path.

The success of their water project in Zambia depended on it.

Monitoring and Controlling Risks

As the sun rose over the camp, casting a golden glow across the landscape, Michael convened the project team for their daily risk management meeting. With a sense of purpose, they gathered around a table covered in charts and reports, ready to assess the effectiveness of their risk mitigation efforts.

1. Reviewing Key Metrics:

Michael began the meeting by reviewing the key metrics tracked since the implementation of their risk mitigation plans.

"Let's start by looking at our flood mitigation efforts. Anna, what's the status of our barriers and drainage systems?"

Anna flipped through her notes before responding, "The barriers are holding up well, and the drainage systems are functioning as intended. So far, we haven't experienced any significant flooding incidents."

2. Assessing Equipment Maintenance:

Natasha provided an update on the equipment maintenance program. "Our technicians have been diligent in adhering to the maintenance schedule, and we haven't encountered any major breakdowns. We've also been able to address minor issues promptly, minimizing downtime."

Michael nodded in approval. "That's good to hear. Our proactive approach seems to be paying off."

3. Monitoring Political Stability:

Peter reported on the political stability in the region. "There haven't been any significant developments that could impact our project. However, we're maintaining close contact with local authorities and staying vigilant."

4. Addressing New Risks:

During the meeting, the team also discussed new risks that had emerged since their last assessment. John raised concerns about potential delays in the delivery of essential materials due to transportation issues.

Michael listened attentively before responding, "Let's proactively address this risk by exploring alternative transportation routes and securing backup suppliers if necessary."

5. Adjusting Mitigation Strategies:

Based on their discussions, the team identified areas where their mitigation strategies could be strengthened. They decided to conduct additional training sessions for equipment maintenance technicians to enhance their skills further.

6. Communication and Documentation:

Before concluding the meeting, Michael emphasized the importance of clear communication and documentation. "Let's ensure that all updates and changes to our risk mitigation plans are communicated promptly to the relevant stakeholders. Detailed documentation will also be essential for future reference."

As the meeting drew to a close, the team dispersed, each member tasked with implementing the decisions made during their discussion. Michael watched them go, a sense of pride swelling within him. Despite the inherent challenges of their project, they were proving themselves capable of managing risks effectively and ensuring the success of their mission in Zambia.

Case Studies in Risk Management

As the project team gathered around the table, Michael introduced a new segment to their risk management meeting: case studies. He believed that learning from real-world examples would provide valuable insights and help strengthen their own risk management practices.

1. Case Study 1:

Michael began by sharing a case study of a similar water project in a neighboring country. "In this case, the project faced unexpected delays due to political unrest in the region. Despite having robust risk mitigation plans in place, the project team struggled to adapt to the rapidly changing situation."

Anna raised her hand. "What lessons can we learn from this?"

Michael nodded. "The key takeaway is the importance of flexibility and adaptability. No matter how well-prepared we are, external factors beyond our control can still impact our project. We need to be agile in our response and have contingency plans in place for any eventuality."

2. Case Study 2:

Natasha shared another case study involving equipment failure during a critical phase of a construction project. "In this scenario, the project team had neglected regular maintenance of their equipment, leading to a breakdown at a crucial moment. As a result, the project faced significant delays and cost overruns."

John interjected, "How can we prevent a similar situation from happening to us?"

Natasha responded, "By prioritizing proactive maintenance and adhering to a strict maintenance schedule, we can minimize the risk of equipment failure. Regular inspections and preventive measures can help identify and address potential issues before they escalate."

3. Case Study 3:

Peter presented a case study involving supply chain disruptions caused by unexpected weather conditions. "In this case, the project team had failed to anticipate the impact of adverse weather on their transportation routes, resulting in delays in the delivery of critical materials."

Michael added, "What can we learn from this?"

Peter replied, "We need to conduct thorough risk assessments of our supply chain and identify alternative transportation routes to mitigate the impact of adverse weather. It's essential to have backup suppliers and contingency plans in place to ensure continuity of operations."

As the team discussed the case studies, they gleaned valuable insights into the complexities of risk management and the importance of proactive planning and adaptability. Armed with this newfound knowledge, they were more confident in their ability to navigate the challenges ahead and ensure the success of their water project in Zambia.

Budgeting and Financial Management

Cost Estimation Techniques

In a cozy conference room at the project headquarters, Michael gathered the project team to discuss the crucial topic of cost estimation. With charts and graphs projected onto the screen, they delved into the various techniques used to estimate project costs.

1. Bottom-Up Estimation:

Michael started the discussion by explaining the bottom-up estimation technique. "With this approach, we break down the project into smaller, more manageable tasks and estimate the costs associated with each one."

Anna, the environmental specialist, nodded in understanding. "This method allows us to account for all the individual components of the project and ensure we don't overlook any expenses."

2. Analogous Estimation:

Natasha, the technical lead, chimed in, "Analogous estimation involves using historical data from similar projects as a basis for estimating costs. It's a quick and relatively simple method, especially when detailed information is not available."

John, the logistics manager, added, "But we need to be

cautious when using this technique, as the accuracy of the estimates relies heavily on the similarity between the current project and past projects."

3. Parametric Estimation:

Peter, the financial advisor, spoke next. "Parametric estimation involves using mathematical models and statistical techniques to extrapolate costs based on certain parameters, such as size, complexity, or quantity."

Michael nodded in agreement. "Parametric estimation can be particularly useful for projects with well-defined parameters, where historical data may not be readily available."

4. Three-Point Estimation:

As the discussion progressed, the team explored the concept of three-point estimation. "Three-point estimation involves estimating three scenarios for each task: the most likely, optimistic, and pessimistic outcomes," Michael explained.

Natasha pointed out, "This method helps us account for uncertainty and variability in project tasks, providing a more realistic range of cost estimates."

5. Expert Judgment:

Finally, Michael highlighted the importance of expert judgment in cost estimation. "Sometimes, despite our best efforts, we need to rely on the expertise and experience of our team members or external consultants to provide accurate cost estimates."

6. Combining Techniques:

Before concluding the meeting, Michael emphasized the value of combining multiple estimation techniques to arrive at more accurate and reliable cost estimates. "By leveraging a variety of approaches, we can mitigate the inherent uncertainties and risks associated with cost estimation."

As the meeting came to an end, the project team felt more equipped to tackle the challenges of budgeting and financial management. Armed with a deeper understanding of cost estimation techniques, they were ready to develop a comprehensive budget that would ensure the success of their water project in Zambia.

8

Chapter 8: Budgeting and Financial Management

Budget Development and Approval

With cost estimation techniques thoroughly discussed, the project team shifted their focus to the critical task of budget development and approval. Gathered around the conference table, they embarked on a meticulous process to allocate resources effectively and ensure financial viability for their water project in Zambia.

1. Reviewing Cost Estimates:

Michael began by presenting the compiled cost estimates based on the various estimation techniques discussed earlier. "Before we proceed with budget development, let's review the cost estimates to ensure accuracy and completeness."

Anna, with her keen eye for detail, meticulously scrutinized the figures, cross-referencing them with the project requirements. "The estimates seem comprehensive, but we should consider including a contingency reserve to account for unforeseen expenses," she suggested.

2. Aligning with Project Objectives:

Natasha emphasized the importance of aligning the budget with the project objectives. "Our budget should reflect the priorities outlined in the project charter and address the critical needs of the communities we aim to serve."

John, nodding in agreement, added, "We should also ensure that the budget allows for flexibility to accommodate changes or unforeseen circumstances that may arise during the project lifecycle."

3. Seeking Stakeholder Input:

Peter proposed involving key stakeholders in the budget development process to garner their input and ensure buy-in. "Engaging stakeholders early on will foster transparency and accountability, ultimately leading to greater support for the project."

Michael nodded in approval. "Let's schedule a meeting with our project sponsors and other relevant stakeholders to present the proposed budget and solicit their feedback."

4. Drafting the Budget Proposal:

Armed with insights from their discussions, the team set to work drafting the budget proposal. They meticulously allocated funds to various project activities, taking into account the cost estimates, project timeline, and resource requirements.

5. Presenting to the Steering Committee:

Once the budget proposal was finalized, Michael scheduled a meeting with the project steering committee to present their recommendations. With charts and graphs illustrating the projected costs and benefits, he eloquently articulated the rationale behind each budget allocation.

6. Securing Approval:

After a thorough review and constructive discussion, the steering committee approved the budget proposal unanimously. Michael breathed a sigh of relief, knowing that their financial plan was robust and aligned with the project's strategic objectives.

As the team celebrated this milestone, they knew that their diligent efforts in budget development and approval had laid a solid foundation for the successful execution of their water project. With financial stability ensured, they were ready to embark on the next phase of their journey with confidence and determination.

Monitoring and Controlling Costs

With the budget approved, the project team shifted their focus to the critical task of monitoring and controlling costs. Gathered once again in the conference room, they devised a robust plan to ensure financial discipline and accountability throughout the project lifecycle.

1. Establishing Baselines:

Michael initiated the discussion by emphasizing the importance of establishing baselines for cost monitoring. "Before we can effectively control costs, we need to establish baseline estimates against which we can measure actual expenditures."

Anna, with her expertise in environmental economics, suggested, "We should establish separate baselines for different cost categories, such as labor, materials, and overheads, to facilitate more granular monitoring."

2. Implementing Cost Tracking Systems:

Natasha, the technical lead, proposed implementing robust cost tracking systems to monitor expenditures in real-time.

"By leveraging project management software, we can track costs against budgeted amounts and identify variances early on."

John, the logistics manager, added, "We should also establish clear procedures for documenting and approving expenses to ensure transparency and accountability."

3. Conducting Regular Budget Reviews:

Peter, the financial advisor, emphasized the importance of conducting regular budget reviews to assess project performance and identify any deviations from the budget. "By conducting periodic reviews, we can proactively address cost overruns or deviations from the budgeted plan."

4. Analyzing Variances:

During the budget reviews, the team meticulously analyzed variances between budgeted and actual costs. They identified root causes for any deviations and developed corrective action plans to bring costs back in line with the budget.

5. Implementing Cost Controls:

Armed with insights from their variance analysis, the team implemented cost controls to prevent future cost overruns. They established spending thresholds, streamlined procurement processes, and negotiated favorable terms with vendors to optimize costs.

6. Communicating Financial Performance:

Finally, Michael emphasized the importance of transparent communication regarding financial performance. "We need to keep stakeholders informed about our financial performance, both positive and negative, to maintain trust and credibility."

As the meeting concluded, the team felt confident in their ability to monitor and control costs effectively throughout the project lifecycle. With robust systems in place and a proactive approach to cost management, they were poised for financial success in their water project in Zambia.

Managing Project Finances

With cost monitoring and control mechanisms in place, the project team shifted their focus to the crucial task of managing project finances. Gathered around the table, they discussed strategies to ensure prudent financial management and optimize resource utilization for their water project in Zambia.

1. Optimizing Resource Allocation:
Michael initiated the discussion by emphasizing the importance of optimizing resource allocation to maximize efficiency and minimize waste. "We need to carefully allocate financial resources, labor, and materials to ensure they are used effectively to achieve project objectives."

Anna, with her expertise in environmental economics, suggested, "We should prioritize investments in sustainable technologies and practices that offer long-term benefits while minimizing environmental impact."

2. Cash Flow Management:
Natasha, the technical lead, emphasized the importance of effective cash flow management to ensure sufficient liquidity for project activities. "We need to maintain a healthy cash flow to meet our financial obligations, such as paying vendors and contractors, without delays."

John, the logistics manager, added, "We should also monitor our accounts receivable and accounts payable to ensure timely invoicing and payment processing."

3. Contingency Planning:
Peter, the financial advisor, highlighted the importance of

120

contingency planning to mitigate financial risks and uncertainties. "We should establish contingency reserves to address unforeseen expenses or changes in project scope that may impact our budget."

4. Cost-Benefit Analysis:

During the discussion, the team conducted a cost-benefit analysis to evaluate the potential return on investment for various project activities and initiatives. They prioritized investments that offered the greatest value and aligned with the project's strategic objectives.

5. Financial Reporting and Transparency:

The team reiterated the importance of transparent financial reporting to stakeholders to maintain trust and accountability. They committed to providing regular updates on project finances, including income statements, balance sheets, and cash flow statements.

6. Compliance and Governance:

Before concluding the meeting, the team discussed the importance of compliance with financial regulations and governance standards. They committed to adhering to relevant laws and regulations and implementing robust internal controls to prevent fraud and financial mismanagement.

As the meeting concluded, the team felt confident in their ability to effectively manage project finances and ensure financial success for their water project in Zambia. With prudent financial management practices in place, they were ready to navigate any financial challenges that may arise and deliver value to their stakeholders.

Financial Reporting and Analysis

With project finances carefully managed, the project team turned their attention to financial reporting and analysis. As they gathered around the table, they discussed strategies to provide transparent and insightful financial information to stakeholders for their water project in Zambia.

1. Establishing Reporting Procedures:

Michael opened the discussion by emphasizing the importance of establishing clear procedures for financial reporting. "We need to define the frequency, format, and content of financial reports to ensure consistency and clarity."

Anna, with her eye for detail, suggested, "We should also establish key performance indicators (KPIs) to measure financial performance and track progress towards our budgeted goals."

2. Generating Financial Statements:

Natasha, the technical lead, outlined the process for generating financial statements, including income statements, balance sheets, and cash flow statements. "Our financial statements should provide a comprehensive view of our financial position, performance, and cash flows."

3. Analyzing Financial Performance:

John, the logistics manager, proposed conducting regular financial analysis to identify trends, patterns, and areas for improvement. "By analyzing our financial performance, we can make informed decisions and take corrective actions to ensure financial success."

4. Budget Variance Analysis:

During the meeting, the team conducted a variance analysis to compare actual financial results with budgeted amounts. They identified variances and investigated root causes to determine whether corrective actions were necessary.

5. Providing Insights to Stakeholders:

Peter, the financial advisor, emphasized the importance of providing insightful financial information to stakeholders. "Our financial reports should not only present the numbers but also provide meaningful insights and explanations to help stakeholders understand our financial performance."

6. Continuous Improvement:

Before concluding the meeting, the team discussed the importance of continuous improvement in financial reporting and analysis processes. They committed to soliciting feedback from stakeholders and refining their reporting practices to enhance transparency and effectiveness.

As the meeting adjourned, the team felt confident in their ability to provide transparent and insightful financial reporting for their water project in Zambia. With robust reporting procedures in place, they were ready to keep stakeholders informed and engaged throughout the project lifecycle.

Case Studies in Budget Management

As the project team delved deeper into the intricacies of budget management, they turned their attention to real-world case studies to gain practical insights and lessons learned. Gathered around the table, they analyzed past projects and their approaches to budget management, drawing inspiration and valuable lessons for their water project in Zambia.

1. Case Study: Clean Water Initiative

The team examined a successful clean water initiative in a rural community, where effective budget management played a crucial role in achieving project objectives. They discussed how the project team meticulously allocated resources, tracked expenditures, and adapted their budget as needed to overcome challenges and deliver clean water to the community.

2. Case Study: Infrastructure Development Project

In another case study, the team analyzed an infrastructure development project that faced budget overruns and delays due to poor financial management practices. They identified key mistakes, such as inadequate cost estimation, ineffective resource allocation, and lack of contingency planning, which led to project setbacks and cost overruns.

3. Lessons Learned:

Reflecting on the case studies, the team identified valuable lessons learned for their own project:

- The importance of thorough cost estimation and budget planning to avoid surprises.
- The need for proactive monitoring and control of project expenditures to prevent budget overruns.
- The value of contingency planning to address unforeseen challenges and changes in project scope.
- The significance of transparent communication and stake-holder engagement regarding project finances.

4. Applying Insights to Their Project:

Armed with insights from the case studies, the team brainstormed ways to apply these lessons to their water project in Zambia. They discussed strategies to enhance budget planning, improve cost estimation techniques, and implement robust monitoring and control mechanisms to ensure financial success.

5. Continuous Learning and Improvement:

The team concluded the discussion by reaffirming their commitment to continuous learning and improvement in budget management practices. They agreed to regularly review their budget performance, analyze variances, and adjust their approach as needed to optimize financial outcomes for their project.

6. Final Thoughts:

As the meeting drew to a close, the team felt empowered by the practical insights gained from the case studies. With a deeper understanding of budget management best practices and potential pitfalls, they were better equipped to navigate the financial aspects of their water project in Zambia and deliver value to the community.

As the team dispersed, they carried with them the invaluable lessons learned from the case studies, eager to apply them in their ongoing project endeavors and contribute to its success.

9

Chapter 9: Quality Management

Defining Quality Standards and Metrics

I n a spacious conference room, the project team gathered
to delve into the crucial aspect of quality management
for their water project in Zambia. With pens poised
and minds focused, they embarked on a journey to define
quality standards and metrics that would guide their pursuit
of excellence.

1. Setting the Stage:
Michael, the project manager, set the stage for the discussion
by highlighting the significance of defining clear quality
standards and metrics. "Quality is paramount in our project.
It's not just about meeting technical specifications but also
about ensuring that our deliverables meet the needs and
expectations of our stakeholders."

2. Understanding Stakeholder Expectations:
Natasha, the technical lead, emphasized the importance of
understanding stakeholder expectations to define appropriate

quality standards. "We need to engage with our stakeholders to identify their requirements and preferences regarding water quality, reliability, and safety."

3. Defining Quality Criteria:

John, the logistics manager, proposed brainstorming sessions to define specific quality criteria for different project deliverables. "We should establish measurable criteria for water quality, infrastructure durability, and service reliability to ensure that our project meets the highest standards."

4. Selecting Quality Metrics:

Anna, with her expertise in environmental engineering, suggested selecting key quality metrics to monitor and measure project performance. "We should identify metrics such as water purity levels, infrastructure integrity, and customer satisfaction ratings to assess our project's quality."

5. Incorporating Best Practices:

Peter, the financial advisor, recommended incorporating industry best practices and regulatory requirements into their quality standards. "We must adhere to relevant quality standards and regulations to ensure compliance and uphold the integrity of our project."

6. Continuous Improvement:

Before concluding the meeting, the team reaffirmed their commitment to continuous improvement in quality management practices. They agreed to regularly review and update their quality standards and metrics based on feedback, lessons learned, and changing project requirements.

As the meeting adjourned, the project team felt energized and empowered by their collective efforts to define clear quality standards and metrics. With a shared vision of excellence, they were ready to embark on their quality management journey and deliver a water project that would transform lives in Zambia.

Quality Planning and Assurance

Continuing their exploration of quality management, the project team delved into the critical aspects of quality planning and assurance for their water project in Zambia. With a shared commitment to excellence, they gathered to develop strategies to ensure that their project would meet the highest standards of quality.

1. Developing a Quality Management Plan:
Michael, the project manager, kicked off the discussion by emphasizing the importance of developing a comprehensive quality management plan. "Our plan should outline how we will implement, monitor, and control quality throughout the project lifecycle."

2. Identifying Quality Assurance Activities:
Natasha, the technical lead, proposed identifying specific quality assurance activities to prevent defects and errors. "We need to establish processes for inspecting materials, testing water samples, and verifying compliance with quality standards."

3. Implementing Quality Control Measures:
John, the logistics manager, suggested implementing quality control measures to identify and address quality issues promptly. "We should conduct regular inspections, audits, and reviews to ensure that our project meets quality requirements and specifications."

4. Training and Empowering Team Members:
Anna, with her background in training and development,

emphasized the importance of training and empowering team members to uphold quality standards. "We must provide training on quality management principles, techniques, and tools to ensure that everyone understands their role in maintaining quality."

5. Engaging Stakeholders in Quality Assurance:

Peter, the financial advisor, highlighted the need to engage stakeholders in quality assurance activities. "We should involve stakeholders in quality reviews, feedback sessions, and inspections to ensure that their expectations are met and their feedback is incorporated into our quality improvement efforts."

6. Continuous Monitoring and Improvement:

Before concluding the meeting, the team reiterated their commitment to continuous monitoring and improvement in quality assurance practices. They agreed to establish feedback loops, conduct regular quality reviews, and implement corrective actions as needed to enhance project quality.

As the meeting came to a close, the project team felt confident in their ability to plan and assure quality for their water project in Zambia. With robust quality management strategies in place, they were poised to deliver a project that would not only meet but exceed stakeholders' expectations.

Quality Control Techniques

In their pursuit of project excellence, the team gathered once again to delve into the realm of quality control techniques. With a keen focus on ensuring the highest standards of quality for their water project in Zambia, they embarked on a journey to explore and implement effective quality control measures.

1. Implementing Inspection Processes:

Michael, the project manager, initiated the discussion by highlighting the importance of implementing robust inspection processes. "We need to establish systematic procedures for inspecting materials, equipment, and construction activities to detect and correct defects early on."

2. Conducting Testing and Sampling:

Natasha, the technical lead, emphasized the need for comprehensive testing and sampling to validate the quality of project deliverables. "We should conduct regular water quality tests, material strength tests, and field inspections to ensure that our project meets established quality standards."

3. Utilizing Statistical Quality Control:

John, the logistics manager, introduced the concept of statistical quality control to the team. "By collecting and analyzing data using statistical techniques, we can identify trends, patterns, and deviations from expected quality levels, enabling us to take proactive measures to maintain quality."

4. Implementing Process Improvement Methods:

Anna, with her expertise in process improvement, suggested implementing continuous improvement methodologies such as Six Sigma and Lean to enhance quality control processes. "By streamlining workflows, eliminating waste, and standardizing procedures, we can improve efficiency and consistency in our project outcomes."

5. Enforcing Quality Standards and Procedures:

Peter, the financial advisor, emphasized the importance of enforcing quality standards and procedures throughout the project lifecycle. "We must ensure that all team members adhere to established quality standards, follow prescribed procedures, and maintain meticulous records to facilitate traceability and accountability."

6. Engaging in Root Cause Analysis:

Before concluding the meeting, the team discussed the importance of conducting root cause analysis to identify and address underlying issues affecting quality. "By digging deep into the root causes of quality issues, we can implement targeted corrective actions to prevent recurrence and continuously improve our project processes."

As the meeting drew to a close, the team felt invigorated by their exploration of quality control techniques. With a comprehensive understanding of these methods, they were ready to implement them effectively to uphold the highest standards of quality for their water project in Zambia.

Tools for Quality Improvement

Gathered around the conference table, the project team delved into the world of quality improvement tools, eager to enhance the quality of their water project in Zambia. Armed with a plethora of techniques and technologies, they embarked on a journey to explore tools that would enable them to achieve optimal project outcomes.

1. Cause and Effect Diagrams:

Michael, the project manager, introduced cause and effect diagrams as a powerful tool for identifying and analyzing root causes of quality issues. "By visually mapping out the relationships between potential causes and their effects, we can gain valuable insights into the factors influencing project quality."

2. Pareto Analysis:

Natasha, the technical lead, explained how Pareto analysis

could help prioritize quality improvement efforts. "By iden-tifying the most significant contributors to quality issues, we can focus our resources on addressing the vital few factors that have the greatest impact on project quality."

3. Control Charts:

John, the logistics manager, demonstrated how control charts could be used to monitor process performance over time. "Control charts enable us to detect variations and trends in project parameters, allowing us to take timely corrective actions to maintain process stability and consistency."

4. Checklists and Templates:

Anna, with her penchant for organization, emphasized the value of checklists and templates in standardizing quality assurance processes. "By providing predefined checklists and templates for quality inspections and audits, we can ensure that essential steps are not overlooked and that quality standards are consistently met."

5. Quality Management Software:

Peter, the financial advisor, introduced quality management software as a comprehensive solution for managing quality-related activities. "Quality management software offers fea-tures such as document control, non-conformance tracking, and corrective action management, enabling us to streamline and automate our quality processes."

6. Benchmarking and Best Practices:

Before concluding the meeting, the team discussed the importance of benchmarking against industry standards and adopting best practices from other successful projects. "By benchmarking our performance against industry leaders and learning from their successes, we can identify opportunities for improvement and strive for excellence in our project."

As the meeting came to a close, the team felt empowered by their exploration of tools for quality improvement. With a diverse arsenal of techniques at their disposal, they were poised to enhance the quality of their water project and deliver lasting value to the communities they served in Zambia.

Conducting Quality Audits

In their pursuit of project excellence, the team convened to discuss the critical process of conducting quality audits for their water project in Zambia. With a commitment to upholding the highest standards of quality, they embarked on a journey to assess and improve the quality of project deliverables through systematic audits.

1. Planning the Audit Process:

Michael, the project manager, outlined the importance of meticulous planning for quality audits. "Before conducting audits, we need to define audit objectives, scope, criteria, and methodologies to ensure that the audit process is thorough and effective."

2. Executing the Audit:

Natasha, the technical lead, emphasized the need for impartiality and objectivity during the audit process. "Auditors should conduct audits systematically, following established procedures and protocols to gather evidence, assess compliance, and identify areas for improvement."

3. Documenting Audit Findings:

John, the logistics manager, highlighted the importance of documenting audit findings accurately and comprehensively. "Auditors should document observations, deviations, and nonconformities discovered during audits, along with recommendations for corrective and preventive actions."

4. Reporting Audit Results:

Anna, with her expertise in communication, stressed the importance of clear and concise reporting of audit results. "Audit reports should provide stakeholders with a detailed summary of audit findings, including strengths, weaknesses, opportunities, and threats, along with recommendations for improvement."

5. Implementing Corrective Actions:

Peter, the financial advisor, discussed the critical role of corrective actions in addressing audit findings. "Upon receiving audit reports, project teams should promptly implement corrective actions to rectify identified issues and prevent their recurrence in future project activities."

6. Follow-Up and Continuous Improvement:

Before concluding the meeting, the team reiterated the importance of follow-up and continuous improvement in the audit process. "By conducting regular audits, implementing corrective actions, and monitoring their effectiveness, we can continuously improve project quality and achieve our quality objectives."

As the meeting came to a close, the team felt empowered by their discussion on conducting quality audits. With a clear understanding of audit processes and methodologies, they were ready to implement audits effectively to enhance the quality of their water project in Zambia.

Continuous Improvement in Project Management

The project team gathered once more, their focus now on the vital concept of continuous improvement in project management. With a commitment to delivering the best possible outcomes for their water project in Zambia, they explored strategies to enhance their processes and practices continually.

1. Embracing a Culture of Learning:

Michael, the project manager, emphasized the importance of fostering a culture of learning within the team. "By encouraging open communication, knowledge sharing, and ongoing training, we can create an environment where team members are motivated to learn and improve."

2. Soliciting Feedback from Stakeholders:

Natasha, the technical lead, suggested actively seeking feedback from project stakeholders to identify areas for improvement. "By soliciting feedback from stakeholders, we can gain valuable insights into their expectations, preferences, and concerns, allowing us to tailor our approach and deliver greater value."

3. Analyzing Performance Metrics:

John, the logistics manager, discussed the significance of analyzing performance metrics to identify trends and patterns. "By regularly monitoring key performance indicators (KPIs) and project metrics, we can identify areas of underperformance or inefficiency and take corrective actions to improve project outcomes."

4. Conducting Lessons Learned Reviews:

Anna, with her penchant for organization, proposed conducting lessons learned reviews at key project milestones. "By reflecting on past experiences, successes, and challenges, we can extract valuable lessons that can inform our future decision-making and improve our project processes."

5. Implementing Best Practices:

Peter, the financial advisor, highlighted the importance of benchmarking against industry best practices. "By studying best practices from other successful projects and adopting proven methodologies, we can leverage existing knowledge and expertise to drive continuous improvement."

6. Iterating and Evolving:

Before concluding the meeting, the team reaffirmed their commitment to iteration and evolution in project management. "Continuous improvement is not a one-time effort but an ongoing journey. By embracing change, iterating on our processes, and evolving with the project, we can adapt to new challenges and opportunities and achieve greater success."

As the meeting drew to a close, the team felt energized by their discussion on continuous improvement. With a shared commitment to learning, feedback, and adaptation, they were poised to elevate their project management practices and deliver exceptional results for their water project in Zambia.

10

Chapter 10: Resource Management

Identifying and Acquiring Resources

As the project progressed, the team gathered to delve into the critical aspect of resource management. With their sights set on ensuring optimal allocation and utilization of resources for their water project in Zambia, they embarked on a discussion to identify and acquire the necessary resources to drive project success.

1. Assessing Resource Requirements:

Michael, the project manager, initiated the discussion by emphasizing the importance of assessing resource requirements. "Before we can acquire resources, we need to conduct a thorough assessment of our project's resource needs, including human, financial, material, and equipment resources."

2. Identifying Resource Constraints:

Natasha, the technical lead, highlighted the significance of identifying potential resource constraints early on in the project lifecycle. "By identifying resource constraints such as budget limitations, skill shortages, and availability constraints, we can proactively address these challenges and mitigate their impact on project delivery."

3. Developing a Resource Plan:

John, the logistics manager, proposed developing a comprehensive resource plan to guide resource allocation and utilization. "A resource plan should outline the types and quantities of resources needed for each project activity, along with timelines and budget allocations to ensure efficient resource management."

4. Acquiring External Resources:

Anna, with her expertise in procurement, discussed strategies for acquiring external resources. "Whether through outsourcing, subcontracting, or procurement, we need to identify reliable suppliers and vendors to provide the resources we need, ensuring quality and cost-effectiveness."

5. Leveraging Internal Resources:

Peter, the financial advisor, emphasized the importance of leveraging internal resources wherever possible. "By maximizing the utilization of internal resources, such as skilled personnel, equipment, and facilities, we can minimize costs and enhance project control and coordination."

6. Establishing Resource Contingency Plans:

Before concluding the meeting, the team discussed the importance of establishing resource contingency plans to mitigate unforeseen resource risks. "By developing contingency plans for resource shortages, delays, or disruptions, we can maintain project continuity and resilience in the face of challenges."

As the meeting adjourned, the team felt equipped with the knowledge and strategies needed to effectively identify and acquire resources for their water project. With a clear plan in place, they were ready to navigate the complexities of resource management and propel their project toward success.

Resource Allocation and Optimization

The project team reconvened to delve deeper into the intricacies of resource management, focusing now on the vital process of resource allocation and optimization. With their water project in Zambia relying heavily on efficient resource utilization, they embarked on a discussion to ensure the optimal allocation of resources to maximize project outcomes.

1. Assessing Resource Availability:

Michael, the project manager, kicked off the discussion by emphasizing the importance of assessing resource availability. "Before we can allocate resources, we need to determine their availability and capacity to ensure we can meet project demands without overburdening our resources."

2. Prioritizing Resource Allocation:

Natasha, the technical lead, stressed the need for prioritization when allocating resources. "We must prioritize resources based on project priorities, critical path activities, and resource dependencies to ensure that essential tasks are adequately resourced and completed on time."

3. Balancing Resource Workloads:

John, the logistics manager, highlighted the significance of balancing resource workloads to prevent overallocation or underutilization. "By balancing resource workloads, we can optimize resource utilization, minimize bottlenecks, and ensure that resources are allocated efficiently across project activities."

4. Adjusting Resource Allocation as Needed:

Anna, with her eye for detail, suggested regularly monitoring and adjusting resource allocations as needed. "Project dynamics can change rapidly, so we need to continuously monitor resource usage and adjust allocations as necessary to adapt to changing project requirements and priorities."

5. Optimizing Resource Utilization:

Peter, the financial advisor, discussed strategies for optimizing resource utilization to maximize efficiency and minimize waste. "By optimizing resource utilization through efficient scheduling, task allocation, and multitasking, we can enhance productivity and reduce project costs."

6. Leveraging Technology for Resource Management:

Before concluding the meeting, the team discussed the role of technology in resource management. "By leveraging project management software and tools for resource planning, scheduling, and tracking, we can streamline resource management processes and improve decision-making."

As the meeting drew to a close, the team felt empowered with the knowledge and strategies needed to effectively allocate and optimize resources for their water project in Zambia. With a renewed focus on efficiency and effectiveness, they were poised to drive their project forward and achieve success.

Managing Human Resources

The project team gathered once more, this time to delve into the critical aspect of managing human resources for their water project in Zambia. With the success of their endeavor reliant on the skills, dedication, and collaboration of their team members, they embarked on a discussion to ensure effective management of human resources throughout the project lifecycle.

1. Recruiting and Staffing:

Michael, the project manager, emphasized the importance of recruiting and staffing the project team with the right talent. "We need to recruit team members with the necessary skills, experience, and expertise to effectively contribute to the project's success."

2. Team Development and Training:

Natasha, the technical lead, highlighted the significance of team development and training. "Investing in the development and training of our team members not only enhances their skills and capabilities but also fosters a culture of learning and continuous improvement."

3. Establishing Clear Roles and Responsibilities:

John, the logistics manager, stressed the need for establishing clear roles and responsibilities within the project team. "By defining clear roles and responsibilities, we can minimize confusion, enhance accountability, and improve overall team effectiveness."

4. Promoting Collaboration and Communication:

Anna, with her knack for organization, discussed strategies for promoting collaboration and communication among team members. "Effective collaboration and communication are essential for project success. By fostering open communication channels and promoting a collaborative culture, we can facilitate information sharing, problem-solving, and decision-making."

5. Managing Team Dynamics:

Peter, the financial advisor, delved into the complexities of managing team dynamics. "Understanding and managing team dynamics, including interpersonal conflicts, divergent opinions, and varying work styles, is crucial for maintaining team cohesion and productivity."

6. Recognizing and Rewarding Performance:

Before concluding the meeting, the team discussed the importance of recognizing and rewarding individual and team performance. "By acknowledging and rewarding exceptional performance, we can boost morale, motivation, and engagement among team members, driving overall project success."

As the meeting came to a close, the team felt equipped with the knowledge and strategies needed to effectively manage human resources for their water project in Zambia. With a focus on recruiting top talent, fostering team development, and promoting collaboration, they were ready to harness the full potential of their human capital and propel their project toward success.

Managing Physical and Financial Resources

The project team reconvened once more, this time to tackle the crucial aspect of managing physical and financial resources for their water project in Zambia. With the success of their endeavor hinging on efficient utilization of both physical assets and financial resources, they embarked on a discussion to ensure effective management of these vital resources throughout the project lifecycle.

1. Procurement and Inventory Management:

Michael, the project manager, initiated the discussion by emphasizing the importance of procurement and inventory management. "We need to carefully manage our procurement processes and inventory to ensure timely acquisition of materials and equipment while minimizing waste and inventory costs."

2. Equipment and Material Handling:

Natasha, the technical lead, highlighted the significance of proper handling and utilization of equipment and materials. "Effective equipment and material handling practices, including storage, transportation, and maintenance, are essential for preventing damage, delays, and cost overruns."

3. Financial Planning and Budget Control:

John, the logistics manager, delved into the complexities of financial planning and budget control. "We need to develop robust financial plans and budgets to guide our spending and ensure that we stay within allocated budgets while maximizing value and minimizing financial risks."

4. Cost Monitoring and Reporting:

Anna, with her eye for detail, discussed strategies for monitoring and reporting costs throughout the project lifecycle. "By implementing rigorous cost monitoring and reporting mechanisms, we can track project expenditures, identify variances, and take corrective actions to keep costs in check."

5. Risk Management for Physical and Financial Resources:

Peter, the financial advisor, stressed the importance of risk management for both physical and financial resources. "Identifying and mitigating risks related to equipment failure, supply chain disruptions, cost overruns, and budget constraints is crucial for safeguarding project resources and ensuring project success."

6. Sustainability and Resource Conservation:

Before concluding the meeting, the team discussed the importance of sustainability and resource conservation in resource management practices. "By promoting sustainable practices and resource conservation measures, we can minimize environmental impact, reduce waste, and enhance long-term project viability."

As the meeting drew to a close, the team felt empowered with the knowledge and strategies needed to effectively manage physical and financial resources for their water project in Zambia. With a renewed focus on procurement efficiency, cost control, and sustainability, they were poised to maximize resource utilization and drive their project toward success.

Resource Scheduling and Leveling

Gathered around the conference table, the project team delved into the intricacies of resource scheduling and leveling for their water project in Zambia. With project success reliant on the efficient allocation and utilization of resources over time, they embarked on a discussion to ensure the optimal scheduling and leveling of resources throughout the project lifecycle.

1. Creating Resource Schedules:
Michael, the project manager, initiated the discussion by emphasizing the importance of creating comprehensive resource schedules. "We need to develop detailed resource schedules that outline the allocation of resources to specific tasks and activities over time, taking into account dependencies and constraints."

2. Identifying Resource Constraints:
Natasha, the technical lead, highlighted the significance of identifying and managing resource constraints. "We must identify resource constraints, such as limited availability of

equipment or specialized skills, and develop strategies to mitigate their impact on project schedules."

3. Smoothing Resource Assignments:

John, the logistics manager, discussed the concept of resource leveling to smooth resource assignments and prevent overallocation or underutilization. "Resource leveling involves adjusting resource assignments to ensure a steady workload over time, minimizing peaks and valleys in resource demand."

4. Balancing Resource Workloads:

Anna, with her keen organizational skills, emphasized the importance of balancing resource workloads. "By balancing resource workloads, we can ensure that resources are utilized efficiently and effectively, preventing burnout and maximizing productivity."

5. Adjusting Schedules as Needed:

Peter, the financial advisor, stressed the need for flexibility in resource scheduling. "Project dynamics can change, requiring adjustments to resource schedules. We must be prepared to adapt and modify schedules as needed to accommodate changing project requirements."

6. Monitoring Resource Utilization:

Before concluding the meeting, the team discussed strategies for monitoring resource utilization to ensure adherence to schedules. "By regularly monitoring resource utilization and comparing actuals to planned allocations, we can identify deviations and take corrective actions to keep the project on track."

As the meeting came to a close, the team felt equipped with the knowledge and strategies needed to effectively schedule and level resources for their water project in Zambia. With a focus on comprehensive resource schedules, efficient resource utilization, and flexibility in scheduling, they were ready to optimize resource allocation and drive their project toward success.

Monitoring and Controlling Resource Usage

In the heart of their project headquarters, the team gathered to delve into the critical aspect of monitoring and controlling resource usage for their water project in Zambia. With the success of their endeavor dependent on the effective oversight of resource utilization, they embarked on a discussion to ensure meticulous monitoring and control of resources throughout the project lifecycle.

1. Establishing Monitoring Mechanisms:

Michael, the project manager, led the discussion by emphasizing the need to establish robust monitoring mechanisms for resource usage. "We must implement monitoring systems to track resource usage in real-time, allowing us to identify deviations from planned allocations and take timely corrective actions."

2. Regular Performance Reviews:

Natasha, the technical lead, emphasized the importance of conducting regular performance reviews to assess resource usage. "Regular performance reviews enable us to evaluate resource utilization against planned allocations, identify inefficiencies or bottlenecks, and implement measures to improve resource efficiency."

3. Implementing Change Control Procedures:

John, the logistics manager, discussed the importance of implementing change control procedures to manage changes in resource usage. "Change control procedures help us assess the impact of changes on resource utilization, evaluate alternative solutions, and make informed decisions to ensure optimal resource allocation."

4. Addressing Resource Overruns:

Anna, with her analytical mindset, delved into strategies for addressing resource overruns. "In cases of resource overruns, we must promptly identify the root causes, assess the impact on project objectives, and implement corrective actions to mitigate risks and bring resource usage back on track."

5. Optimizing Resource Allocation:

Peter, the financial advisor, stressed the need to continuously optimize resource allocation. "By analyzing resource usage patterns, identifying opportunities for optimization, and reallocating resources as needed, we can ensure that resources are utilized efficiently and effectively throughout the project lifecycle."

6. Reporting and Communication:

Before concluding the meeting, the team discussed the importance of regular reporting and communication regarding resource usage. "Transparent reporting and communication regarding resource usage enable stakeholders to stay informed, make data-driven decisions, and ensure alignment with project goals and objectives."

As the meeting drew to a close, the team felt empowered with the knowledge and strategies needed to effectively monitor and control resource usage for their water project in Zambia. With a focus on establishing robust monitoring mechanisms, conducting regular performance reviews, and implementing change control procedures, they were poised to optimize resource utilization and drive their project toward success.

11

Chapter 11: Procurement Management

Developing a Procurement Plan

A round the conference table, the project team gathered to delve into the intricacies of procurement management for their water project in Zambia. With the success of their endeavor contingent on the effective acquisition of goods and services, they embarked on a discussion to develop a comprehensive procurement plan.

1. Assessing Procurement Needs:

Michael, the project manager, initiated the discussion by emphasizing the importance of assessing procurement needs. "Before we can develop a procurement plan, we must conduct a thorough assessment of our procurement needs, including materials, equipment, and services required for project implementation."

2. Defining Procurement Requirements:

Natasha, the technical lead, stressed the need to define clear procurement requirements. "Clear and detailed procurement requirements help us communicate our needs to potential suppliers and ensure that their proposals align with project objectives and specifications."

3. Identifying Potential Suppliers:

John, the logistics manager, delved into strategies for identifying potential suppliers. "We need to identify and evaluate potential suppliers based on factors such as expertise, reputation, cost, and capacity to meet our procurement needs."

4. Developing Procurement Strategies:

Anna, with her keen strategic mindset, discussed the importance of developing procurement strategies. "Procurement strategies outline the approach we will take to acquire goods and services, including sourcing methods, contract types, and negotiation strategies."

5. Establishing Procurement Procedures:

Peter, the financial advisor, emphasized the need to establish clear procurement procedures. "Well-defined procurement procedures ensure consistency, transparency, and compliance with regulatory requirements throughout the procurement process."

6. Documenting the Procurement Plan:

Before concluding the meeting, the team discussed the importance of documenting the procurement plan. "Documenting the procurement plan ensures that all team members are aligned on procurement objectives, strategies, and procedures, facilitating smooth execution and accountability."

As the meeting came to a close, the team felt equipped with the knowledge and strategies needed to develop a procurement plan for their water project in Zambia. With a focus on assessing procurement needs, defining requirements, and identifying potential suppliers, they were ready to embark on the procurement process and drive their project toward success.

Identifying Procurement Needs

Seated around the table, the project team delved into the crucial task of identifying procurement needs for their water project in Zambia. With the success of their endeavor reliant on acquiring the necessary materials, equipment, and services, they engaged in a discussion to ensure a thorough understanding of their procurement requirements.

1. Analyzing Project Scope:

Michael, the project manager, initiated the discussion by emphasizing the importance of analyzing the project scope to identify procurement needs. "To identify our procurement needs, we must first analyze the project scope to determine the materials, equipment, and services required for project implementation."

2. Conducting Needs Assessment:

Natasha, the technical lead, stressed the need to conduct a comprehensive needs assessment. "A needs assessment involves evaluating project requirements, considering factors such as technical specifications, quality standards, and regulatory compliance to determine our procurement needs accurately."

3. Engaging Stakeholders:

John, the logistics manager, highlighted the importance of engaging stakeholders in the procurement needs identification process. "Stakeholder engagement is crucial for gathering input, clarifying requirements, and ensuring alignment between project objectives and procurement needs."

4. Prioritizing Procurement Requirements:

Anna, with her meticulous attention to detail, discussed strategies for prioritizing procurement requirements. "Prioritizing procurement requirements helps us allocate resources effectively, focus on critical needs, and ensure that procurement activities align with project priorities."

5. Anticipating Future Needs:

Peter, the financial advisor, emphasized the need to anticipate future needs when identifying procurement requirements. "We must anticipate future project phases, changes in project scope, and emerging requirements to ensure that our procurement plan is flexible and adaptable to evolving project needs."

6. Documenting Procurement Needs:

Before concluding the meeting, the team discussed the importance of documenting procurement needs for reference and transparency. "Documenting procurement needs ensures that all stakeholders have a clear understanding of project requirements and facilitates communication with potential suppliers during the procurement process."

As the meeting drew to a close, the team felt confident in their ability to identify procurement needs effectively for their water project in Zambia. With a focus on analyzing project scope, conducting needs assessments, and engaging stakeholders, they were ready to proceed with developing a comprehensive procurement plan to support project success.

Vendor Selection and Contract Management

In the bustling project office, the team gathered to tackle the critical task of vendor selection and contract management for their water project in Zambia. With the success of their endeavor hinging on securing reliable suppliers and establishing robust contracts, they delved into a discussion to ensure meticulous vendor selection and effective contract management.

1. Identifying Potential Vendors:

Michael, the project manager, kicked off the discussion by emphasizing the importance of identifying potential vendors. "To select the right vendors, we need to conduct thorough research, gather recommendations, and evaluate supplier qualifications based on factors such as experience, capabilities, and reputation."

2. Evaluating Vendor Proposals:

Natasha, the technical lead, delved into strategies for evaluating vendor proposals. "We must carefully review vendor proposals, assess their alignment with project requirements, and consider factors such as pricing, quality, delivery timelines, and contractual terms before making a selection."

3. Negotiating Contracts:

John, the logistics manager, highlighted the significance of negotiating contracts with selected vendors. "Negotiating contracts allows us to clarify terms, define expectations, and ensure mutual understanding and agreement on deliverables, timelines, payment terms, and other key aspects of the partnership."

4. Establishing Performance Metrics:

Anna, with her analytical mindset, discussed the importance

of establishing performance metrics within contracts. "Including performance metrics in contracts enables us to monitor vendor performance, track progress, and hold vendors accountable for meeting agreed-upon standards and milestones."

5. Managing Contracts Effectively:

Peter, the financial advisor, emphasized the need to manage contracts effectively throughout their lifecycle. "Effective contract management involves ongoing monitoring, compliance checks, and proactive resolution of issues to ensure that contracts deliver value, mitigate risks, and support project success."

6. Mitigating Contractual Risks:

Before concluding the meeting, the team discussed strategies for mitigating contractual risks. "Identifying potential risks, incorporating risk mitigation measures into contracts, and establishing contingency plans help us safeguard project interests and minimize the impact of unforeseen challenges."

As the meeting came to a close, the team felt empowered with the knowledge and strategies needed to navigate vendor selection and contract management for their water project in Zambia. With a focus on identifying potential vendors, evaluating proposals, and negotiating contracts, they were ready to forge partnerships that would support project success.

Managing Supplier Relationships

Gathered around the conference table, the project team delved into the crucial topic of managing supplier relationships for their water project in Zambia. Recognizing that strong supplier relationships are essential for project success, they engaged in a discussion to explore strategies for fostering positive partnerships with their vendors.

1. Establishing Open Communication Channels:

Michael, the project manager, emphasized the importance of establishing open communication channels with suppliers. "Maintaining transparent and regular communication with our suppliers is key to building trust, addressing issues promptly, and ensuring alignment on project goals and expectations."

2. Setting Clear Expectations:

Natasha, the technical lead, stressed the need to set clear expectations with suppliers from the outset. "We must communicate our project requirements, specifications, and quality standards clearly to suppliers to avoid misunderstandings and ensure that deliverables meet our expectations."

3. Providing Feedback and Recognition:

John, the logistics manager, discussed the importance of providing feedback and recognition to suppliers. "Recognizing suppliers for their contributions and providing constructive feedback fosters a positive working relationship, encourages continuous improvement, and reinforces our commitment to collaboration."

4. Resolving Issues Promptly:

Anna, with her problem-solving skills, highlighted the importance of resolving issues promptly. "When issues arise, we must address them swiftly, collaborate with suppliers to find solutions, and prevent them from escalating to avoid disruptions to project timelines and deliverables."

5. Building Long-Term Partnerships:

Peter, the financial advisor, emphasized the benefits of building long-term partnerships with suppliers. "Investing in long-term relationships with reliable suppliers fosters stability, promotes loyalty, and opens opportunities for collaboration, innovation, and mutual growth."

6. Conducting Performance Reviews:

Before concluding the meeting, the team discussed the importance of conducting regular performance reviews with suppliers. "Evaluating supplier performance against established metrics allows us to identify strengths, areas for improvement, and opportunities for collaboration to enhance project outcomes."

As the meeting drew to a close, the team felt equipped with the strategies needed to manage supplier relationships effectively for their water project in Zambia. With a focus on open communication, clear expectations, and proactive issue resolution, they were ready to cultivate strong partnerships that would support project success.

Procurement Risk Management

Seated around the table, the project team delved into the critical aspect of procurement risk management for their water project in Zambia. Recognizing the inherent risks associated with procurement activities, they engaged in a discussion to identify, assess, and mitigate potential risks to ensure successful project delivery.

1. Identifying Procurement Risks:

Michael, the project manager, initiated the discussion by emphasizing the importance of identifying procurement risks. "We need to conduct a comprehensive risk assessment to identify potential risks associated with procurement activities, including supplier failure, cost overruns, quality issues, and supply chain disruptions."

2. Assessing Risk Impact and Probability:

Natasha, the technical lead, stressed the need to assess the impact and probability of identified risks. "By analyzing the potential impact and likelihood of occurrence for each procurement risk, we can prioritize our risk mitigation efforts and allocate resources effectively to address high-priority risks."

3. Developing Risk Mitigation Strategies:

John, the logistics manager, discussed strategies for mitigating procurement risks. "We must develop risk mitigation strategies tailored to each identified risk, including contingency planning, alternative sourcing options, contract provisions, and supplier diversification to reduce the likelihood and impact of adverse events."

4. Monitoring and Control Measures:

Anna, with her attention to detail, highlighted the importance of implementing monitoring and control measures. "Continuous monitoring of procurement activities, regular risk reviews, and proactive risk response planning enable us to identify emerging risks, assess their impact, and implement timely mitigation measures to safeguard project objectives."

5. Contingency Planning:

Peter, the financial advisor, emphasized the need for contingency planning in procurement risk management. "Developing contingency plans and allocating reserves for unforeseen events ensure that we have a proactive response strategy in place to address unexpected challenges and minimize their impact on project outcomes."

6. Lessons Learned and Continuous Improvement:

Before concluding the meeting, the team discussed the importance of learning from past experiences and continuously improving procurement risk management practices. "By conducting post-project reviews, capturing lessons learned, and incorporating feedback into our procurement processes, we can enhance our risk management capabilities and strengthen project resilience."

As the meeting concluded, the team felt equipped with the knowledge and strategies needed to effectively manage procurement risks for their water project in Zambia. With a focus on risk identification, assessment, mitigation, and continuous improvement, they were ready to navigate procurement challenges and ensure project success.

Measuring Procurement Performance

Seated around the table, the project team delved into the crucial aspect of measuring procurement performance for their water project in Zambia. Understanding that effective measurement is essential for evaluating the efficiency and effectiveness of procurement activities, they engaged in a discussion to identify key performance indicators (KPIs) and metrics for assessing procurement performance.

1. Defining Key Performance Indicators (KPIs):

Michael, the project manager, initiated the discussion by emphasizing the importance of defining KPIs for measuring procurement performance. "We need to identify and define KPIs that align with our project objectives and procurement goals, such as cost savings, supplier performance, delivery timeliness, and contract compliance."

2. Tracking Cost Savings and Cost Avoidance:

Natasha, the technical lead, stressed the need to track cost savings and cost avoidance achieved through procurement activities. "By comparing actual procurement costs against budgeted costs, analyzing cost variances, and quantifying cost savings and cost avoidance, we can assess the financial impact of our procurement initiatives."

3. Evaluating Supplier Performance:

John, the logistics manager, discussed the importance of evaluating supplier performance. "Monitoring supplier performance against predefined criteria, such as quality, delivery performance, responsiveness, and compliance with contractual terms, allows us to identify top-performing suppliers, address underperforming suppliers, and optimize supplier relationships."

4. Assessing Procurement Cycle Time:

Anna, with her analytical mindset, highlighted the significance of assessing procurement cycle time. "Measuring the time taken to complete procurement activities, from requisition to contract award and delivery, enables us to identify bottlenecks, streamline processes, and improve procurement efficiency."

5. Monitoring Contract Compliance:

Peter, the financial advisor, emphasized the need for monitoring contract compliance. "Tracking adherence to contractual terms, including pricing agreements, delivery schedules, quality standards, and service level agreements, ensures that suppliers fulfill their obligations and mitigates contractual risks."

6. Conducting Periodic Performance Reviews:

Before concluding the meeting, the team discussed the importance of conducting periodic performance reviews to assess procurement performance. "Regular performance reviews allow us to evaluate progress, identify areas for improvement, and make data-driven decisions to optimize procurement processes and outcomes."

As the meeting drew to a close, the team felt equipped with the tools and strategies needed to measure procurement performance effectively for their water project in Zambia. With a focus on defining KPIs, tracking cost savings, evaluating supplier performance, assessing cycle time, monitoring contract compliance, and conducting performance reviews, they were ready to optimize procurement processes and achieve project success.

12

Chapter 12: Project Execution

Directing and Managing Project Work

In the heart of their project site in Zambia, amidst the bustling sounds of construction and the fervent energy of the team, Michael, the project manager, gathered his team to discuss the crucial phase of project execution. With a clear goal of translating plans into action, they delved into the intricacies of directing and managing project work.

1. Setting Clear Direction:

Michael stood tall, his voice cutting through the ambient noise. "Now is the time to set our direction clearly. Each team member needs to understand their role, responsibilities, and the project's overall objectives."

2. Establishing Communication Channels:

Natasha, the technical lead, emphasized the importance of open communication. "We must establish effective communication channels to ensure seamless information flow between team members, stakeholders, and external partners."

3. Managing Resources Efficiently:

John, the logistics manager, nodded in agreement. "Resource management is critical during execution. We need to ensure that materials, equipment, and manpower are allocated efficiently to avoid delays and bottlenecks."

4. Adhering to Quality Standards:

Anna, with her meticulous eye for detail, reminded the team of the importance of quality. "We cannot compromise on quality. Every task, every component must meet the highest standards to ensure the longevity and effectiveness of our project."

5. Monitoring Progress Continuously:

Peter, the financial advisor, stressed the need for continuous monitoring. "We must track progress closely, identifying any deviations from the plan and taking corrective action promptly to keep the project on track."

6. Anticipating and Managing Risks:

As the discussion progressed, the team acknowledged the inevitability of risks during execution. "We must be proactive in identifying potential risks and have mitigation strategies in place to address them before they escalate," Michael affirmed.

With their roles clarified, communication channels established, resources optimized, quality standards upheld, progress monitored, and risks mitigated, the team felt a renewed sense of determination as they prepared to embark on the execution phase of their project. In the sweltering heat of Zambia, they were ready to turn plans into reality and bring their vision to life.

Implementing Project Plans

With the blueprint of their project spread out before them, the team shifted their focus to the meticulous task of implementing their meticulously crafted plans. In the bustling project site of Zambia, amidst the clatter of machinery and the buzz of activity, Michael, the project manager, led the team in discussing the intricate process of bringing their plans to life.

1. Translating Plans into Action:

Michael's voice cut through the noise as he addressed the team. "Now is the time to put our plans into action. Each team member has a vital role to play in executing their assigned tasks with precision and dedication."

2. Ensuring Adherence to Timeline:

Natasha, the technical lead, stressed the importance of time management. "We must adhere to our project timeline rigorously. Any delays could have cascading effects on subsequent tasks and ultimately impact project completion."

3. Coordination and Collaboration:

John, the logistics manager, emphasized the need for seamless coordination. "Effective collaboration between different teams and departments is crucial. We must work together cohesively to ensure smooth execution and avoid conflicts."

4. Quality Control Measures:

Anna, with her keen eye for detail, highlighted the significance of quality control. "Every aspect of our project must meet the highest quality standards. We must implement stringent quality control measures to detect and rectify any deviations from the set standards."

5. Flexibility and Adaptability:

Peter, the financial advisor, acknowledged the unpredictable nature of project execution. "We must remain flexible and adaptable to unforeseen challenges or changes in circumstances. Our ability to pivot and adjust our plans as needed will be critical to success."

6. Real-time Monitoring and Reporting:

As the discussion progressed, the team emphasized the importance of real-time monitoring and reporting. "We must track progress continuously, identify any issues or deviations promptly, and communicate updates transparently to stakeholders," Michael affirmed.

With their plans set in motion, the team felt a surge of determination as they embarked on the implementation phase of their project. Amidst the cacophony of construction, they worked tirelessly, each action bringing them one step closer to realizing their shared vision in the heart of Zambia.

Managing Project Changes

In the dynamic environment of their project site in Zambia, the team gathered to discuss the inevitable aspect of project management: change. With plans set in motion and progress underway, Michael, the project manager, led the discussion on effectively managing changes to ensure project success.

1. Embracing Change:

Michael's voice resonated with conviction as he addressed the team. "Change is inevitable in any project. Instead of resisting it, we must embrace change as an opportunity for improvement and innovation."

2. Assessing Impact:

Natasha, the technical lead, emphasized the importance of assessing the impact of proposed changes. "Before implementing any change, we must thoroughly analyze its potential effects on the project timeline, budget, and overall objectives."

3. Prioritizing Changes:

John, the logistics manager, stressed the need to prioritize changes based on their urgency and significance. "Not all changes are created equal. We must prioritize changes based on their impact on project deliverables and stakeholder expectations."

4. Communicating Changes Effectively:

Anna, with her knack for clear communication, highlighted the importance of transparent communication. "We must communicate changes promptly and clearly to all stakeholders, ensuring everyone is on the same page and understands the reasons behind the proposed changes."

5. Adapting Plans Accordingly:

Peter, the financial advisor, underscored the need to adapt plans accordingly. "Once changes are approved, we must update our project plans and adjust our resources, timelines, and budgets accordingly to accommodate the new requirements."

6. Documenting Changes:

As the discussion unfolded, the team emphasized the importance of documentation. "Every change, its rationale, and its impact must be meticulously documented to maintain a clear record of project evolution and decision-making processes," Michael concluded.

Armed with a proactive mindset and a structured approach to managing changes, the team felt empowered to navigate the dynamic landscape of their project site in Zambia. Amidst the whirlwind of activity, they stood united, ready to adapt and thrive in the face of change.

Ensuring Team Collaboration and Coordination

As the project progressed amidst the bustling activity of the Zambia project site, Michael, the project manager, gathered the team to discuss the critical aspect of collaboration and coordination. With various tasks and timelines intricately intertwined, the team recognized the importance of seamless teamwork.

1. Fostering Open Communication:

Michael's voice resonated with authority as he addressed the team. "Open communication is the cornerstone of effective collaboration. We must encourage transparent communication channels to ensure everyone is informed and aligned."

2. Establishing Clear Roles and Responsibilities:

Natasha, the technical lead, emphasized the need for clarity in roles and responsibilities. "Each team member must understand their role and responsibilities within the project framework. Clear delineation of duties minimizes confusion and maximizes efficiency."

3. Leveraging Technology for Collaboration:

John, the logistics manager, highlighted the role of technology in facilitating collaboration. "We have access to a myriad of collaboration tools that can streamline communication and enhance productivity. Leveraging these tools effectively will facilitate seamless teamwork."

4. Regular Team Meetings:

Anna, with her eye for detail, stressed the importance of regular team meetings. "Scheduled team meetings provide a forum for discussing progress, addressing concerns, and aligning on next steps. These meetings foster a sense of unity and purpose among team members."

5. Cross-Functional Integration:

Peter, the financial advisor, emphasized cross-functional integration. "Our project involves multiple departments and disciplines. We must promote cross-functional collaboration to leverage diverse perspectives and expertise for optimal outcomes."

6. Resolving Conflicts Constructively:

As the discussion unfolded, the team acknowledged the inevitability of conflicts. "Conflicts may arise, but they must be addressed constructively and resolved promptly to prevent disruption to project progress," Michael concluded.

Empowered by a shared commitment to collaboration and coordination, the team returned to their respective tasks with renewed vigor. Amidst the orchestrated chaos of the project site, they worked in harmony, each action contributing to the collective success of their endeavor in Zambia.

Monitoring Progress and Performance

With the project in full swing, Michael, the project manager, gathered the team to discuss the crucial aspect of monitoring progress and performance. Amidst the flurry of activity on the Zambia project site, it was imperative to maintain a keen eye on key metrics to ensure project success.

1. Establishing Key Performance Indicators (KPIs):

Michael's voice commanded attention as he addressed the team. "To gauge our progress effectively, we must establish clear KPIs that align with our project objectives. These metrics will serve as benchmarks for assessing our performance."

2. Real-Time Monitoring Tools:

Natasha, the technical lead, highlighted the role of real-time monitoring tools. "We have access to advanced monitoring tools that provide real-time insights into project progress. Leveraging these tools allows us to identify potential issues early and take corrective action promptly."

3. Regular Progress Reviews:

John, the logistics manager, stressed the importance of regular progress reviews. "Scheduled progress reviews provide an opportunity to assess our performance against established KPIs, identify areas for improvement, and recalibrate our strategies accordingly."

4. Performance Analysis and Reporting:

Anna, with her meticulous approach, emphasized the need for performance analysis and reporting. "We must conduct thorough performance analysis to identify trends, patterns, and outliers. Clear and concise reporting enables us to communicate progress effectively to stakeholders."

5. Addressing Deviations from Plan:

Peter, the financial advisor, underscored the importance of addressing deviations from the plan. "If we encounter deviations from our planned targets, we must investigate the root causes and take corrective action promptly to realign with our project objectives."

6. Continuous Improvement:

As the discussion unfolded, the team embraced the concept of continuous improvement. "By continuously monitoring our progress and performance, we can identify opportunities for improvement and implement enhancements to optimize our project outcomes," Michael concluded.

Armed with a proactive approach to monitoring progress and performance, the team returned to their tasks with renewed determination. Each action taken was guided by a shared commitment to excellence, driving them closer to the successful completion of their project in Zambia.

Addressing Issues and Roadblocks

In the midst of the bustling activity on the Zambia project site, Michael, the project manager, convened the team to discuss the critical aspect of addressing issues and roadblocks. With the complexity of the project, challenges were inevitable, but proactive management was essential to keep the project on track.

1. Identifying Potential Issues:

Michael's voice cut through the din as he addressed the team. "We must maintain a vigilant eye for potential issues that could impede our progress. Early identification allows us to address them before they escalate into major roadblocks."

2. Rapid Response Mechanisms:

Natasha, the technical lead, emphasized the need for rapid response mechanisms. "When issues arise, we must have predefined protocols in place for swift resolution. Clear escalation paths and designated points of contact ensure that issues are addressed promptly."

3. Collaborative Problem-Solving:

John, the logistics manager, highlighted the power of collaborative problem-solving. "Addressing complex issues often requires input from multiple stakeholders. By fostering a collaborative environment, we can tap into the collective wisdom of the team to find innovative solutions."

4. Flexibility and Adaptability:

Anna, with her pragmatic approach, stressed the importance of flexibility. "In the face of unforeseen challenges, we must be willing to adapt our plans and strategies. Flexibility allows us to navigate obstacles with agility and resilience."

5. Resource Reallocation:

Peter, the financial advisor, underscored the role of resource reallocation. "When confronted with roadblocks, we may need to reallocate resources to overcome challenges. Prioritizing critical tasks and reallocating resources accordingly ensures that we maintain momentum."

6. Continuous Improvement:

As the discussion progressed, the team embraced the concept of continuous improvement. "Every challenge we encounter presents an opportunity for learning and growth," Michael concluded. "By addressing issues proactively and learning from our experiences, we strengthen our ability to overcome future obstacles."

Empowered by a shared commitment to proactive problem-solving, the team returned to their tasks with renewed determination. Each roadblock they encountered was not seen as a setback, but rather as a stepping stone on their journey to project success in Zambia.

Chapter 13: Monitoring and Controlling

Tracking Project Progress

As the Zambia project entered a crucial phase, Michael, the project manager, gathered the team to discuss the vital aspect of tracking project progress. With timelines to meet and stakeholders to satisfy, it was imperative to keep a close eye on every aspect of the project's development.

1. Establishing Baselines:

Michael's authoritative voice commanded attention as he addressed the team. "Before we can track progress, we must establish baselines for key project parameters. These baselines will serve as benchmarks against which we can measure our actual performance."

2. Utilizing Project Management Software:

Natasha, the technical lead, emphasized the role of project management software in tracking progress. "Our project management software provides real-time visibility into project progress. By inputting data and updating tasks regularly, we can ensure that everyone stays informed and aligned."

3. Regular Status Meetings:

John, the logistics manager, stressed the importance of regular status meetings. "Scheduled status meetings provide an opportunity to review progress, discuss any issues or road-blocks, and adjust plans accordingly. Clear communication is key to keeping everyone on the same page."

4. Milestone Tracking:

Anna, with her meticulous attention to detail, highlighted the significance of milestone tracking. "Breaking the project down into smaller milestones allows us to track progress more effectively. Celebrating the achievement of milestones boosts morale and keeps the team motivated."

5. Performance Measurement:

Peter, the financial advisor, underscored the importance of performance measurement. "We must track not only progress but also performance against key metrics. By analyzing performance data, we can identify trends, spot potential issues, and take corrective action as needed."

6. Continuous Monitoring and Adaptation:

As the discussion unfolded, the team embraced the concept of continuous monitoring and adaptation. "Monitoring progress is not a one-time activity," Michael concluded. "It requires constant vigilance and a willingness to adapt our plans as circumstances change."

Armed with a robust system for tracking progress, the team returned to their tasks with renewed focus and determination. Each update entered into the project management software brought them one step closer to achieving their goals in Zambia.

Performance Measurement Techniques

With the Zambia project progressing steadily, Michael, the project manager, convened the team to delve into the intricacies of performance measurement techniques. Understanding how to gauge the project's performance would be crucial in ensuring its success.

1. Key Performance Indicators (KPIs):

Michael began by emphasizing the importance of identifying and tracking key performance indicators (KPIs). "KPIs serve as quantifiable metrics that allow us to measure the success of our project against predefined objectives," he explained. "They provide valuable insights into our progress and areas that require attention."

2. Earned Value Management (EVM):

Natasha, the technical lead, elaborated on the concept of earned value management (EVM). "EVM integrates cost, schedule, and scope to provide a holistic view of project performance," she elucidated. "By comparing the planned value, earned value, and actual costs, we can assess our project's performance and forecast future outcomes."

3. Variance Analysis:

John, the logistics manager, introduced the team to the concept of variance analysis. "Variance analysis involves comparing actual performance against planned performance to identify deviations," he explained. "By analyzing the reasons behind these variances, we can take corrective actions to keep the project on track."

4. Performance Reviews:

Anna, with her keen eye for detail, emphasized the importance of regular performance reviews. "Performance reviews provide an opportunity to evaluate individual and team performance," she noted. "They foster accountability, encourage continuous improvement, and ensure alignment with project objectives."

5. Customer Satisfaction Surveys:

Peter, the financial advisor, highlighted the significance of customer satisfaction surveys. "Ultimately, the success of our project hinges on meeting the needs and expectations of our stakeholders," he emphasized. "Conducting customer satisfaction surveys allows us to gather feedback, identify areas for improvement, and enhance overall project performance."

6. Benchmarking:

As the discussion concluded, the team recognized the value of benchmarking against industry standards and best practices. "Benchmarking provides valuable insights into how our project performance compares to that of similar projects," Michael concluded. "It enables us to identify opportunities for improvement and strive for excellence."

Armed with a comprehensive understanding of performance measurement techniques, the team returned to their tasks with renewed confidence. Each performance metric they tracked brought them one step closer to achieving project excellence in Zambia.

Earned Value Management (EVM)

In the heart of their project journey, Michael, the project manager, gathered the team to dive deep into the complexities of Earned Value Management (EVM). Understanding this technique would provide them with a comprehensive view of their project's performance.

1. Understanding EVM Fundamentals:

Michael began by breaking down the fundamentals of EVM. "Earned Value Management integrates cost, schedule, and scope to evaluate project performance," he explained. "It allows us to measure project progress objectively and predict future outcomes."

2. Key EVM Metrics:

Natasha, the technical lead, elaborated on the key metrics used in EVM. "There are three primary metrics: Planned Value (PV), Earned Value (EV), and Actual Cost (AC)," she clarified. "PV represents the authorized budget for work scheduled, EV is the value of work performed, and AC is the actual cost incurred."

3. Calculating EVM Metrics:

John, the logistics manager, demonstrated how to calculate these metrics using a hypothetical example. "By comparing EV to PV, we can determine Schedule Performance Index (SPI), and comparing EV to AC gives us Cost Performance Index (CPI)," he explained. "SPI and CPI help us assess schedule and cost performance, respectively."

4. Interpreting EVM Results:

Anna, with her analytical mindset, emphasized the importance of interpreting EVM results. "A CPI or SPI value of 1 indicates that we are on track, while values below 1 signify potential issues," she noted. "Values above 1 indicate that we are performing better than planned."

5. Forecasting with EVM:

Peter, the financial advisor, highlighted how EVM enables forecasting. "EVM allows us to forecast project completion dates and final costs based on current performance trends," he pointed out. "It helps us anticipate potential risks and take proactive measures to mitigate them."

6. Leveraging EVM for Decision-Making:

As the discussion concluded, the team recognized the value of leveraging EVM for informed decision-making. "EVM provides us with valuable insights into project performance," Michael concluded. "By harnessing this data, we can make strategic decisions to keep our project on track and ensure its success."

Armed with a solid understanding of Earned Value Management, the team returned to their tasks with a newfound appreciation for the power of objective project evaluation. Each calculation brought them closer to achieving their goals in Zambia.

Change Control Process

As the project progressed, Michael, the project manager, convened the team to discuss the vital topic of change control. Understanding how to manage changes effectively would be crucial in ensuring project success.

1. Defining Change Control:

Michael began by defining change control as the process of managing changes to project scope, schedule, and resources. "Change is inevitable in any project," he emphasized. "However, it's essential to have a structured approach to evaluate, approve, and implement changes."

2. Change Request Identification:

Natasha, the technical lead, elaborated on how change requests are identified. "Change requests can arise from various sources, including stakeholders, team members, or external factors," she explained. "It's crucial to have a formal process in place to capture and document these requests."

3. Change Impact Assessment:

John, the logistics manager, highlighted the importance of conducting a thorough impact assessment for each change request. "We need to evaluate the potential effects of proposed changes on project scope, schedule, cost, quality, and risks," he noted. "This helps us make informed decisions and prioritize changes accordingly."

4. Change Review and Approval:

Anna, with her eye for detail, discussed the process of reviewing and approving change requests. "Once a change request is submitted, it undergoes a formal review process," she explained. "The change control board evaluates the request based on predefined criteria and decides whether to approve, reject, or defer it."

5. Change Implementation:

Peter, the financial advisor, emphasized the importance of managing change implementation effectively. "Approved changes must be communicated to relevant stakeholders, and adjustments to project plans must be made accordingly," he stated. "It's essential to track and monitor the implementation of approved changes to ensure they achieve the desired outcomes."

6. Change Control Documentation:

As the discussion concluded, the team recognized the importance of maintaining comprehensive documentation throughout the change control process. "Documenting all change requests, decisions, and their impacts ensures transparency and accountability," Michael concluded. "It also provides a valuable historical record for future reference."

Armed with a solid understanding of the change control

process, the team returned to their tasks with confidence, knowing they could effectively manage changes and keep the project on track in Zambia.

Issue and Defect Management

As the project progressed, Michael, the project manager, recognized the importance of addressing issues and defects promptly to maintain project momentum. Gathering the team, he initiated a discussion on effective issue and defect management.

1. Identifying Issues and Defects:

Michael began by stressing the importance of proactive issue and defect identification. "Issues and defects can arise at any stage of the project," he explained. "It's essential to have mechanisms in place to identify and capture them as soon as they occur."

2. Logging and Prioritizing:

Natasha, the technical lead, emphasized the need for a systematic approach to logging and prioritizing issues and defects. "Each issue or defect should be logged in a centralized system," she suggested. "They should then be prioritized based on their impact on project objectives and timelines."

3. Investigating Root Causes:

John, the logistics manager, highlighted the importance of investigating the root causes of issues and defects. "Understanding why issues and defects occur is crucial for implementing effective solutions," he noted. "Root cause analysis helps us address underlying problems rather than just treating symptoms."

4. Developing Remediation Plans:

Anna, with her analytical skills, discussed the process of developing remediation plans. "Once the root causes are identified, we can develop action plans to address them," she explained. "These plans should outline specific steps, responsibilities, and timelines for resolving issues and defects."

5. Implementing Corrective Actions:

Peter, the financial advisor, emphasized the importance of timely corrective action implementation. "Corrective actions should be implemented promptly to prevent issues and defects from escalating," he stated. "Effective communication and coordination are essential to ensure that corrective actions are executed efficiently."

6. Monitoring and Closure:

As the discussion concluded, the team recognized the importance of ongoing monitoring and closure of issues and defects. "We need to track the progress of corrective actions and verify that they have been effective," Michael concluded. "Closure should only occur once issues and defects have been fully resolved and validated."

Armed with a comprehensive approach to issue and defect management, the team returned to their tasks with renewed vigor, knowing they could address challenges effectively and keep the project on track in Zambia.

Reporting and Dashboard Tools

With the project progressing steadily, Michael, the project manager, gathered the team to discuss the importance of effective reporting and dashboard tools for monitoring project performance.

1. Generating Relevant Reports:

Michael emphasized the need for generating reports that provide relevant and timely information to stakeholders. "Reports should capture key metrics, progress updates, and any deviations from the project plan," he explained. "They should be tailored to the needs of different stakeholders, ensuring they receive the information they require."

2. Utilizing Dashboard Tools:

Natasha, the technical lead, introduced the team to dashboard tools for visualizing project data. "Dashboards offer a real-time overview of project performance," she stated. "They allow stakeholders to quickly assess project health, identify trends, and make informed decisions."

3. Customizing Dashboards:

John, the logistics manager, highlighted the importance of customizing dashboards to suit the preferences of different stakeholders. "Dashboards should be configurable to display relevant metrics and KPIs for each stakeholder group," he suggested. "This ensures that everyone receives the information they need to make informed decisions."

4. Ensuring Accessibility:

Anna, with her focus on stakeholder engagement, discussed the importance of ensuring the accessibility of reports and dashboards. "Reports should be easily accessible to all stakeholders, regardless of their location or device," she explained. "This promotes transparency and collaboration across the project team."

5. Analyzing Trends and Patterns:

Peter, the financial advisor, emphasized the value of analyzing trends and patterns in project data. "By analyzing historical data and trends, we can identify potential risks and opportunities," he noted. "This allows us to proactively adjust our strategies and plans to ensure project success."

6. Continuous Improvement:

As the discussion concluded, the team recognized the importance of continuously improving reporting and dashboard tools based on feedback and lessons learned. "Our goal is to ensure that our reporting mechanisms evolve to meet the changing needs of our stakeholders," Michael concluded.

Armed with powerful reporting and dashboard tools, the team returned to their tasks with confidence, knowing they could effectively monitor and control project performance in Zambia.

14

Chapter 14: Project Closure

Closing Project Phases

As the water project in Zambia neared its completion, Michael, the project manager, convened a meeting to discuss the importance of closing project phases.

1. Reviewing Phase Deliverables:

Michael began by emphasizing the need to review the deliverables of each project phase. "Before closing a phase, we need to ensure that all deliverables have been completed satisfactorily," he explained. "This includes verifying that objectives have been met and quality standards have been upheld."

2. Documenting Phase Closure:

Natasha, the technical lead, highlighted the importance of documenting the closure of each project phase. "We need to maintain comprehensive records of phase closure activities," she stated. "This includes documenting any lessons learned, unresolved issues, and final approvals."

3. Obtaining Stakeholder Sign-Off:

John, the logistics manager, discussed the process of obtaining stakeholder sign-off for phase closure. "Stakeholder sign-off confirms their acceptance of phase deliverables and their readiness to proceed to the next phase," he noted. "It's essential for ensuring alignment and accountability."

4. Transitioning to the Next Phase:

Anna, with her focus on stakeholder engagement, emphasized the importance of smooth transitions between project phases. "As we close one phase, we need to prepare for the transition to the next," she explained. "This includes communicating changes, updating plans, and aligning resources."

5. Conducting Phase Reviews:

Peter, the financial advisor, discussed the value of conducting phase reviews to assess performance and identify areas for improvement. "Phase reviews provide an opportunity to reflect on our achievements and challenges," he stated. "They inform our approach for future phases and projects."

6. Celebrating Milestones:

As the discussion concluded, the team recognized the importance of celebrating milestones and achievements at the close of each project phase. "Celebrating milestones boosts morale and reinforces team spirit," Michael concluded. "It's an opportunity to acknowledge everyone's hard work and dedication."

With a clear understanding of the importance of closing project phases, the team returned to their tasks with renewed focus, eager to bring the water project in Zambia to a successful conclusion.

Conducting Project Evaluations and Reviews

As the final stages of the water project in Zambia unfolded, Michael, the project manager, emphasized the significance of conducting thorough project evaluations and reviews.

1. Assessing Project Performance:

Gathered around a table, the team delved into a discussion on assessing project performance. "We need to evaluate how well we've met project objectives and delivered value to our stakeholders," Michael stressed. "This includes analyzing project metrics, such as schedule adherence, budget variance, and quality outcomes."

2. Reviewing Lessons Learned:

Sarah, the procurement specialist, highlighted the importance of reviewing lessons learned from the project. "Identifying what worked well and what could have been improved is essential for continuous learning and improvement," she remarked. "It enables us to replicate successes and avoid pitfalls in future projects."

3. Conducting Stakeholder Feedback Sessions:

John, the logistics manager, suggested conducting stakeholder feedback sessions to gather insights on project performance. "Stakeholder feedback provides valuable perspectives on our project delivery," he noted. "It helps us understand stakeholder satisfaction and identify areas for enhancement."

4. Analyzing Project Documentation:

Anna, the community liaison officer, emphasized the need to analyze project documentation as part of the evaluation process. "Reviewing project documentation, such as meeting minutes, status reports, and change requests, provides a comprehensive view of project activities," she explained. "It allows us to identify discrepancies and ensure compliance with project requirements."

5. Identifying Best Practices:

Peter, the financial advisor, suggested identifying best practices that emerged during the project. "Recognizing and documenting best practices enables us to institutionalize successful approaches for future projects," he pointed out. "It fosters a culture of continuous improvement and innovation within the organization."

6. Documenting Project Closure:

As the meeting drew to a close, Michael emphasized the importance of documenting project closure activities. "Documenting project evaluations and reviews ensures that valuable insights are captured and shared across the organization," he concluded. "It serves as a foundation for enhancing project management practices and delivering greater value in future endeavors."

Armed with a comprehensive understanding of the importance of project evaluations and reviews, the team set out to apply their insights to ensure the successful closure of the water project in Zambia.

Documenting Lessons Learned

With the project nearing its conclusion, Michael, the project manager, gathered his team to discuss the critical task of documenting lessons learned from their experiences in executing the water project in Zambia.

1. Reflecting on Challenges and Successes:

Gathered around a whiteboard, the team delved into a reflective session, recalling the challenges they faced and the successes they achieved throughout the project journey. "It's essential to capture both the triumphs and the obstacles we encountered," Michael emphasized. "This comprehensive reflection will guide us in refining our approach in future endeavors."

2. Identifying Key Takeaways:

As the discussion progressed, Sarah, the procurement specialist, shared her insights. "We need to distill our experiences into actionable takeaways," she suggested. "Identifying key lessons learned will enable us to make informed decisions and mitigate risks in future projects."

3. Documenting Best Practices:

John, the logistics manager, highlighted the importance of documenting best practices. "Documenting the strategies and techniques that led to success will serve as a roadmap for future projects," he remarked. "It ensures that we build upon our strengths and capitalize on proven approaches."

4. Analyzing Root Causes:

Anna, the community liaison officer, emphasized the need to analyze the root causes of challenges encountered. "Understanding the underlying reasons behind our setbacks is crucial for preventing their recurrence," she explained. "It empowers us to address systemic issues and enhance our project management capabilities."

5. Incorporating Stakeholder Feedback:

Peter, the financial advisor, suggested incorporating stakeholder feedback into the lessons learned documentation. "Stakeholder perspectives provide invaluable insights into areas for improvement," he noted. "By integrating their feedback, we demonstrate our commitment to delivering value and fostering positive relationships."

6. Documenting Actionable Recommendations:

As the meeting concluded, Michael tasked each team member with documenting actionable recommendations based on their insights. "Our lessons learned document should not only capture our experiences but also outline concrete steps for improvement," he stated. "This collective effort will position us for greater success in future projects."

Armed with a comprehensive understanding of their project experiences, the team embarked on the task of documenting their lessons learned, ensuring that their knowledge and insights would inform and inspire future endeavors.

Finalizing Project Documentation

As the project neared its completion, Michael, the project manager, convened a final meeting with his team to ensure the thoroughness of their project documentation.

1. Reviewing Comprehensive Documentation:

Seated around a conference table strewn with project reports and files, the team meticulously reviewed the comprehensive documentation compiled throughout the project lifecycle. Charts, graphs, and narratives painted a vivid picture of the project's journey, capturing its triumphs, challenges, and key milestones.

2. Ensuring Accuracy and Completeness:

With a keen eye for detail, Sarah, the project coordinator, meticulously scrutinized each document to ensure accuracy and completeness. "Our project documentation must reflect the entirety of our efforts," she emphasized. "It serves as a valuable resource for stakeholders and future project teams."

3. Incorporating Lessons Learned:

John, the technical lead, highlighted the importance of integrating lessons learned into the project documentation. "Our experiences provide valuable insights for future projects," he noted. "By documenting our lessons learned, we contribute to the continuous improvement of project management practices."

4. Finalizing Reports and Presentations:

Anna, the communications specialist, focused on finalizing reports and presentations for stakeholders. "Our project documentation is a testament to our dedication and expertise," she remarked. "It's essential to present our findings and achievements in a clear and compelling manner."

5. Archiving Project Files:

As the meeting drew to a close, Peter, the financial analyst, discussed the importance of archiving project files for future reference. "Preserving our project documentation ensures that our knowledge and insights endure beyond the project's completion," he stated. "It lays the foundation for building upon our successes in future endeavors."

6. Celebrating Achievements:

With a sense of pride and accomplishment, the team reflected on their collective achievements throughout the project journey. "Our project documentation is a testament to our resilience, teamwork, and commitment to excellence," Michael remarked. "Let's take a moment to celebrate our successes before we embark on our next endeavors."

With their project documentation finalized and their achievements celebrated, the team stood poised to close the chapter on their current project while eagerly anticipating the opportunities that lay ahead.

Releasing Project Resources

With the project nearing its conclusion, Michael, the project manager, turned his attention to releasing project resources in an organized and efficient manner.

1. Reviewing Resource Allocation:

Gathering his team in the project's command center, Michael reviewed the current allocation of resources. "As we transition out of this project, it's essential to ensure that our resources are appropriately released and reallocated," he emphasized.

2. Identifying Surplus Resources:

With meticulous attention to detail, Sarah, the resource manager, conducted a thorough assessment to identify any surplus resources. "We must avoid wastage and ensure that all resources are utilized effectively," she explained.

3. Notifying Stakeholders:

Anna, the communications specialist, took charge of notifying stakeholders about the release of project resources. "Clear communication is key to managing expectations and ensuring a smooth transition," she remarked as she prepared to disseminate the necessary notifications.

4. Returning Borrowed Equipment:

John and Peter, the technical and financial leads respectively, collaborated to facilitate the return of any borrowed equipment or assets. "Returning borrowed equipment in a timely manner demonstrates our commitment to responsible resource management," John noted.

5. Updating Resource Records:

As resources were released, the team diligently updated resource records to reflect the changes. "Accurate record-keeping is essential for maintaining transparency and accountability," Sarah remarked, ensuring that every change was meticulously documented.

6. Expressing Gratitude:

Before dispersing, Michael took a moment to express his gratitude to the team for their dedication and hard work throughout the project. "Your efforts have been instrumental in our success," he said, acknowledging their contributions. "As we release our project resources, let's carry forward the lessons learned and apply them to our future endeavors."

With their project resources released and their efforts recognized, the team prepared to conclude their project with a sense of accomplishment and readiness for new challenges ahead.

Celebrating Success and Recognizing Contributions

As the project neared its official closure, Michael, the project manager, organized a special gathering to celebrate the team's achievements and recognize their invaluable contributions.

1. Reflecting on Successes:

Gathered in the conference room adorned with project milestones and achievements, the team took a moment to reflect on their journey. "Each of you played a vital role in our success," Michael began, prompting smiles and nods of agreement from his team.

2. Acknowledging Contributions:

With genuine appreciation in his voice, Michael called upon each team member to share their proudest moments and highlights from the project. As stories of collaboration and innovation unfolded, it became evident how each contribution had shaped the project's outcome.

3. Awarding Certificates of Excellence:

To formally recognize their efforts, Michael presented each team member with a personalized certificate of excellence. "Your dedication, creativity, and resilience have been truly remarkable," he remarked as he handed out the certificates, eliciting heartfelt applause and cheers.

4. Sharing Words of Gratitude:

Taking the floor once more, Michael expressed his heartfelt gratitude to the team for their unwavering commitment and exceptional teamwork. "Together, we have overcome challenges, exceeded expectations, and delivered outstanding results," he declared, his words echoing the sentiments of the entire team.

5. Commemorating the Journey:

As a token of remembrance, Michael unveiled a commemorative plaque engraved with the project's name and key milestones. "May this plaque serve as a symbol of our collective achievements and the bonds we've forged along the way," he said, inviting the team to gather for a group photo beside the plaque.

6. Looking Towards the Future:

Amidst laughter and camaraderie, the team toasted to their success and shared aspirations for future endeavors. "While our project may be coming to a close, our journey together is far from over," Michael concluded, his gaze filled with optimism and pride.

With hearts full of pride and memories to cherish, the team bid farewell to their project, knowing that their legacy of excellence would endure long after the final chapter had closed.

15

Chapter 15: Advanced Topics and Future Trends

Project Management in Digital Transformation

As organizations increasingly embrace digital transformation to stay competitive in today's fast-paced world, the role of project management becomes more critical than ever.

1. Embracing Digital Disruption:

In a bustling conference hall, project managers from diverse industries gathered to explore the intersection of project management and digital transformation. With the rapid advancement of technology reshaping business landscapes, the need to adapt and innovate has never been more pressing.

2. Understanding the Digital Landscape:

As the keynote speaker took the stage, he painted a vivid picture of the digital landscape, highlighting the transformative power of technologies such as artificial intelligence, machine learning, and blockchain. "To thrive in the digital age, organizations must harness the potential of these technologies to drive innovation and create value," he emphasized.

3. Integrating Agile Practices:

During interactive workshops, project managers delved into the principles of agile methodologies and their application in digital transformation initiatives. Through collaborative exercises and real-world case studies, they explored how agile practices enable organizations to respond swiftly to changing market dynamics and customer needs.

4. Leveraging Data Analytics:

In a breakout session on data-driven decision-making, project managers learned how harnessing the power of data analytics can drive strategic insights and inform project strategies. From predictive analytics to sentiment analysis, they discovered innovative ways to leverage data to mitigate risks and capitalize on opportunities.

5. Navigating Change Management:

Amidst the excitement of digital transformation, project managers also delved into the challenges of change management. Through candid discussions and interactive simulations, they explored strategies for fostering organizational buy-in, managing resistance to change, and cultivating a culture of innovation.

6. Envisioning the Future:

As the conference drew to a close, project managers left with a renewed sense of purpose and a vision for the future of project management in the digital era. Armed with new insights and tools, they were ready to embark on their digital transformation journeys, poised to lead their organizations to greater heights of success.

With the digital revolution in full swing, project managers

emerged from the conference equipped with the knowledge and skills needed to navigate the complexities of digital transformation and drive meaningful change in their organizations.

The Role of AI and Machine Learning in Project Management

In the bustling corridors of a tech conference, project managers congregated to explore the transformative potential of artificial intelligence (AI) and machine learning (ML) in project management.

1. Embracing AI and ML:

As the keynote speaker took the stage, she captivated the audience with tales of AI and ML revolutionizing project management. From predictive analytics to automated task scheduling, the possibilities seemed endless. "AI and ML aren't just buzzwords; they're reshaping the way we plan, execute, and monitor projects," she proclaimed.

2. Enhancing Decision-Making:

In breakout sessions, project managers delved into the practical applications of AI and ML in project decision-making. Through case studies and hands-on demonstrations, they learned how AI-powered algorithms could analyze vast datasets to identify trends, predict project risks, and optimize resource allocation, empowering project teams to make informed decisions with confidence.

3. Automating Repetitive Tasks:

With the rise of AI-powered project management tools, project managers discovered newfound efficiencies in their workflows. From automating routine administrative tasks to streamlining project communication, AI and ML technologies promised to free up valuable time and resources, allowing teams to focus on higher-value activities that drive project success.

4. Personalizing Project Experiences:

As the day progressed, project managers explored how AI and ML could personalize project experiences for stakeholders. From customized project dashboards to personalized task recommendations, AI-driven insights promised to enhance collaboration, foster engagement, and drive project outcomes.

5. Managing Project Risks:

In a panel discussion on risk management, project managers debated the role of AI and ML in identifying and mitigating project risks. While AI-powered predictive analytics offered unprecedented insights into potential risks, they cautioned against overreliance on technology, emphasizing the importance of human judgment and experience in navigating complex project environments.

6. Looking to the Future:

As the conference drew to a close, project managers left with a newfound appreciation for the transformative potential of AI and ML in project management. With AI-powered tools becoming increasingly ubiquitous, they were eager to embrace the future and harness the power of technology to drive project success in the digital age.

Armed with newfound insights and inspiration, project managers departed the conference with a renewed sense of purpose and a vision for the future of project management powered by AI and machine learning.

Sustainability and Green Project Management

Amidst the lush greenery of a sustainability expo, project managers gathered to explore the intersection of sustainability and project management, eager to discover innovative approaches to promoting environmental stewardship in their projects.

1. Embracing Sustainability:

As the keynote speaker took the stage, she painted a compelling vision of sustainability as a cornerstone of modern project management. "In an era of climate change and resource scarcity, sustainability isn't just a nice-to-have—it's a business imperative," she declared, urging project managers to embrace sustainability principles in their projects.

2. Integrating Green Practices:

In breakout sessions, project managers delved into practical strategies for integrating green practices into project management. From sustainable procurement and energy-efficient design to waste reduction and carbon offsetting, they explored a myriad of ways to minimize environmental impact and maximize sustainability throughout the project lifecycle.

3. Leveraging Renewable Resources:

With the rise of renewable energy technologies, project managers discovered new opportunities to harness the power of nature in their projects. From solar panels and wind turbines to geothermal heating and rainwater harvesting, they explored innovative ways to incorporate renewable resources into project designs, reducing reliance on fossil fuels and promoting environmental sustainability.

4. Engaging Stakeholders:

In a workshop on stakeholder engagement, project managers discussed the importance of involving stakeholders in sustainability initiatives. From community outreach and stakeholder consultations to sustainability reporting and transparency, they explored strategies for building stakeholder buy-in and fostering a culture of sustainability within project teams and organizations.

5. Measuring Environmental Impact:

As the day progressed, project managers delved into the intricacies of measuring environmental impact in projects. From carbon footprint assessments and life cycle analyses to environmental impact assessments and sustainability metrics, they learned how to quantify the environmental consequences of their projects and track progress towards sustainability goals.

6. Looking Ahead:

As the expo drew to a close, project managers left with a newfound commitment to integrating sustainability into their projects. With climate change posing increasingly urgent challenges, they were inspired to lead the charge towards a more sustainable future, leveraging the power of project management to drive positive environmental change and create a greener, more sustainable world for future generations.

With a renewed sense of purpose and a wealth of new insights, project managers departed the sustainability expo ready to embark on a new chapter in project management— one defined by a commitment to sustainability, environmental stewardship, and a greener, more sustainable future.

Project Management in a Global Context

In the bustling metropolis of New York City, project managers from around the world converged for an international conference on project management in a global context. Against the backdrop of towering skyscrapers and bustling streets, they gathered to explore the challenges and opportunities of managing projects across borders and cultures.

1. Embracing Cultural Diversity:

As the conference kicked off, speakers emphasized the importance of embracing cultural diversity in global project management. From understanding cultural norms and communication styles to navigating language barriers and time zones, project managers learned how to leverage cultural differences as a source of strength and creativity in their projects.

2. Building Cross-Cultural Teams:

In breakout sessions, project managers delved into the intricacies of building and leading cross-cultural teams. From fostering trust and collaboration to resolving conflicts and building consensus, they explored strategies for harnessing the unique perspectives and talents of team members from diverse cultural backgrounds.

3. Adapting to Local Contexts:

With case studies from around the world, project managers gained insights into the importance of adapting project management practices to local contexts. From regulatory requirements and legal frameworks to socio-economic conditions and political landscapes, they learned how to navigate the complexities of global project environments and drive successful project outcomes.

4. Leveraging Technology for Global Collaboration:

In a workshop on technology-enabled collaboration, project managers explored the latest tools and technologies for facilitating global collaboration. From project management software and virtual collaboration platforms to video conferencing and instant messaging, they discovered how technology can bridge geographical distances and bring global project teams closer together.

5. Managing Risk in Global Projects:

As the conference continued, project managers delved into the challenges of managing risk in global projects. From geopolitical instability and currency fluctuations to supply chain disruptions and cultural misunderstandings, they learned how to identify, assess, and mitigate risks in a global context, ensuring project success in an increasingly interconnected world.

6. Embracing Globalization:

As the conference drew to a close, project managers reflected on the transformative power of globalization in shaping the future of project management. From expanding market opportunities and fostering innovation to driving economic growth and cultural exchange, they embraced the opportunities and challenges of managing projects in a rapidly evolving global landscape.

Armed with new insights and perspectives, project managers departed the international conference inspired to lead their teams with confidence and agility in an increasingly globalized world. With a shared commitment to collaboration, innovation, and cultural understanding, they looked forward to shaping the future of project management on a global scale.

Future Skills for Project Managers

In a sleek, futuristic conference center nestled among the towering skyscrapers of Singapore, project managers gathered for a symposium on the future skills needed to excel in their profession. Against a backdrop of cutting-edge technology and innovative thinking, they delved into the key competencies that would drive success in the ever-evolving landscape of project management.

1. Adaptability and Resilience:

As the symposium kicked off, speakers emphasized the importance of adaptability and resilience in the face of rapid change. With technological advancements and market disruptions reshaping industries at an unprecedented pace, project managers learned how to embrace uncertainty, pivot quickly, and thrive in dynamic environments.

2. Digital Literacy and Data Analytics:

In breakout sessions, project managers delved into the importance of digital literacy and data analytics in driving project success. From mastering project management software and digital collaboration tools to harnessing the power of data analytics for informed decision-making, they explored how technology could enhance efficiency and effectiveness in project execution.

3. Strategic Thinking and Business Acumen:

With case studies from successful projects around the world, project managers gained insights into the importance of strategic thinking and business acumen in driving project success. From aligning projects with organizational goals and objectives to understanding market dynamics and competitive landscapes, they learned how to think strategically and drive value for their stakeholders.

4. Emotional Intelligence and Leadership Skills:

In a workshop on emotional intelligence and leadership skills, project managers explored the critical role of soft skills in effective project management. From building strong relationships and fostering trust to inspiring and motivating team members, they honed their leadership abilities and learned how to navigate interpersonal dynamics with empathy and grace.

5. Creativity and Innovation:

As the symposium continued, project managers delved into the importance of creativity and innovation in driving project success. From generating innovative ideas and solutions to fostering a culture of experimentation and learning, they discovered how to harness the power of creativity to overcome challenges and seize opportunities in their projects.

6. Lifelong Learning and Continuous Improvement:

With a focus on lifelong learning and continuous improvement, project managers concluded the symposium with a commitment to staying abreast of emerging trends and evolving best practices in project management. From attending workshops and conferences to pursuing professional certifications and networking with peers, they embraced a mindset of continuous growth and development in their profession.

Armed with new skills and perspectives, project managers departed the symposium inspired to lead their teams with confidence and agility in the fast-paced world of project management. With a shared commitment to adaptability, innovation, and lifelong learning, they looked forward to shaping the future of their profession and driving success in projects of all sizes and complexities.

Emerging Trends and Innovations in Project Management

In a bustling innovation hub in Silicon Valley, project management thought leaders and industry pioneers gathered for a symposium on emerging trends and innovations shaping the future of their profession. Against a backdrop of cutting-edge technology and forward-thinking ideas, they explored the latest developments revolutionizing project management practices.

1. Agile Beyond Software Development:
As the symposium kicked off, speakers highlighted the expanding role of Agile methodologies beyond software development. From Agile marketing and sales to Agile HR and finance, project managers learned how Agile principles could be applied across diverse industries and functions to drive innovation and accelerate business outcomes.

2. Hybrid Project Management Approaches:
In breakout sessions, project managers delved into the rise of hybrid project management approaches blending traditional and Agile methodologies. With case studies from successful projects, they explored how hybrid approaches offered the flexibility to adapt to varying project requirements and deliver value in dynamic environments.

3. Remote Project Management and Virtual Collaboration:
With the global shift to remote work, project managers embraced the challenges and opportunities of managing projects in virtual environments. From leveraging collaboration tools and virtual communication platforms to fostering team cohesion and engagement across geographies, they discovered new

strategies for success in the digital age.

4. Artificial Intelligence and Automation:

In a workshop on artificial intelligence and automation, project managers explored how emerging technologies were reshaping project management processes. From AI-powered project planning and scheduling to automated risk assessment and decision support systems, they learned how to harness the power of AI to streamline workflows and drive efficiency.

5. Blockchain and Decentralized Project Management:

As the symposium continued, project managers delved into the potential of blockchain technology to revolutionize project management practices. From decentralized project governance and smart contracts to immutable project records and transparent supply chains, they explored how blockchain could enhance trust, transparency, and accountability in project execution.

6. Sustainability and Ethical Project Management:

With a focus on sustainability and ethical project management, project managers concluded the symposium with a commitment to driving positive social and environmental impact through their projects. From integrating sustainability goals into project objectives to adopting ethical procurement practices and stakeholder engagement strategies, they embraced a holistic approach to project management that prioritized people, planet, and profit.

Inspired by the insights and innovations shared at the symposium, project managers left Silicon Valley energized and equipped to lead their teams with confidence in an era of unprecedented change and disruption. With a shared vision of leveraging emerging trends and technologies to drive positive outcomes for their organizations and society at large, they looked forward to shaping the future of project management and making a lasting impact in their respective fields.

About the Author

Goodson Mumba is a multifaceted individual known for his diverse expertise and prolific contributions across various fields. As an infopreneur, thought leader, and spiritual leader, he has inspired countless individuals through his insightful teachings and impactful writings. Mumba is also an accomplished author, with several notable works to his name, including "Understanding Corporate Worship," "The Years I Spent in a Week," "Management By Harmony," "The CEO's Diary," "Change to Change" and "Creative Thinking for results" His literary works span topics ranging from business management to personal development and spirituality, reflecting his broad range of interests and insights.

With a Master of Business Leadership (MBL) and a Bachelor of Arts in Theology (BTh), Mumba brings a unique blend of business acumen and spiritual wisdom to his work. His educational background is further enriched by a Group Diploma in Management Studies, providing him with a solid foundation in organizational dynamics and leadership principles. Additionally, Mumba holds diplomas in Education Psychology, Leadership and Management Styles, Organizational Behaviour, Financial Accounting, Economic Growth and Development, and Project Management, showcasing his commitment to continuous learning and professional development.

Mumba's expertise extends beyond traditional academic disciplines, encompassing areas such as Neuro-Linguistic Programming (NLP) and Positive Psychology. His diverse skill set is complemented by a range of certifications, including Creative Problem Solving and Decision Making, Life Coaching Fundamentals and Techniques, Professional Life Coaching, and Performance Management System Design. These certifications reflect Mumba's dedication to equipping himself with the tools and knowledge necessary to empower others and drive positive change.

As an author, Mumba's writings reflect his deep understanding of human nature, organizational dynamics, and spiritual principles. His works offer practical insights, actionable strategies, and inspirational guidance for individuals seeking personal growth, professional success, and spiritual fulfillment. Mumba's holistic approach to life and leadership resonates with readers worldwide, making him a respected figure in both the business and spiritual communities.

Overall, Goodson Mumba's diverse background, extensive knowledge, and profound insights make him a sought-after speaker, mentor, and author. His commitment to excellence, lifelong learning, and service to others continues to inspire individuals to unlock their full potential and lead lives of purpose and significance.

Goodson Mumba is renowned for initiating the concept of Management by Harmony, revolutionizing traditional management practices with a focus on balanced and holistic approaches. He has authored two influential books on this subject: "Introduction to Management by Harmony" and its sequel, "Management by Harmony."

Mumba's work has significantly impacted the field, offering innovative strategies for fostering organizational harmony and efficiency. His contributions continue to shape contemporary management theories and practices.